THE PRACTICE CO

Beautiful and inlcusive devotions to lead you to your truest self.
By Liz Milani

VOLUME 03

WELCOME

Attention is the beginning of devotion, wrote Mary Oliver. There is so much going on in the world, and in your life, that it can be a challenge to give any one thing or person or moment your full attention. Devotion is more than reading a two-minute five-point lesson on how to do right and be right and get it right. The spiritual practice of paying attention is about opening your heart and life to the divinity all around, in you, and the divinity that comes through you, too. It takes courage to open your heart, and your eyes, to look and listen and feel long enough to to be attentive. And I know - cos' I'm right here with you on this journey - that it's often easier and more comfortable to pay less attention to the pain and the joy and the nuance and the complexity and the wonder of it all. But you only really to start to live when you sink down deep into the life you already have, where you are, being who you are. And friend, don't you want to live as full and as deep and as true as you can?

This is not your typical devotional. I haven't written it in a way to tell you what you need to do to get to where you want to go. Rather, I want these words to be a friend to you, to be alongside you as you realise that you are enough, you have enough, and you were created with the power and capacity to rise like a phoenix and engage life in all the forms it comes to you in. Just as much as there is to be afraid and wary of in this world, there is so much to love, much love that longs to find you, and so much life waiting for you already, inside your own. Each series within these pages has seven parts. You could read them day by day, binge them all at once, or come and go as you please. Whatever works for you. It's a visual journey as well as a reading one, and there's plenty of room for you to draw in the margins, spill coffee on the words, or tear pages out to give to loved ones. I hope this book brings you courage, grace, and hope. All the love, always, Liz. xo.

FURTHER MORE:

Check out our Daily Devotional App for iOS and Android at **thepracticeco.com/app**

Follow us on Instagram: **@thepracticeco**

Website: **thepracticeco.com**

Grammar and Spelling: **Australian English**

TABLE OF CONTENTS

"WEAR GRATITUDE LIKE
A CLOAK, AND IT WILL
FEED EVERY CORNER OF
YOUR LIFE."

Rumi

THERE IS MORE FOR YOU - PART 1
Abundance As Flow

Do you want more?

Do you believe that there is more for you? More love, joy, adventure, lessons, beauty, wonder, and hope?

What is it that you want more of?

What do you want that you currently don't have?

What lengths would you go to, to get it?

In his memoir, Luke recorded that Jesus said:
"Give generously, and generous gifts will be given back to you, shaken down to make room for more. Abundant gifts will pour out upon you with such an overflowing measure that it will run over the top! Your measurement of generosity becomes the measurement of your return."
(1.)

Perhaps you were taught that the key to getting more was to make sure you were tithing to your local church. 10%, no less; that's how you unlock the windows of heaven over your life. You must give and give and give, time, money, effort, energy, when you have and even when you don't, when it's easy, and especially when it's hard, otherwise, God won't be able to bless you with that 'abundant more' that the scriptures speak of. In this sense, abundance and 'more' is transactional, conditional; to get it, we must do 'this' and 'that.'

Abundance is not quid pro quo - you scratch God's back, and God will scratch yours. Abundance is what happens when you're in sync, in flow; when you're in alignment with divinity. It may sound like splitting hairs, but when you view abundance like it's a zero-sum game, there is never enough to go around, and you better get in quick so that you don't miss out; you better play the game right so that you win, and you get the prize, and you end up with more.

If abundance is what happens when you're in divine flow, there will always be enough, even if you don't have enough, even if you feel like you're always losing.

In Ancient Hebrew, one of the words for abundance is 'shefa,' which is also the word for 'flow.' There is a constant flow of life-giving energy, an abundance of life, that we can tap into if we decide to.

Because that's what abundance is. A decision, not a result. A river, not a game. An awakening, not a transaction.

Jesus said to his friends:
"I have come to give you everything in abundance, more than you expect, life in its fullness until you overflow!"
(2.)

Jesus wasn't giving his friends his top ten tips for getting wealthy. He was showing them that there is a way to live in flow with abundance no matter what you have, no matter where you are. Remember, Jesus was a Rabbi who's people group and nation were forcibly living under the oppression and rule of a foreign military superpower. They were being exploited at every turn - taxed up to 90% of their income, sold into slavery, slaughtered for stealing what they needed to survive. Jesus wasn't speaking to The Forbes 400, he was speaking to the victims of tyrannical profiteering.

"I have come to give you everything in abundance..."

It had nothing to do with their bank accounts. True abundance isn't based on your net worth. It's based on your self-worth.

So, tell me:
What is it that you want?
And what lengths would you go to, to get it?

Mindful Prompt: Take a moment, get comfortable, drop your shoulders, loosen your jaw, breathe deep into your belly, close your eyes. Explore what you want. Ask yourself the question and observe what comes up for you. What does the idea of abundance bring up in your body and heart?

THERE IS MORE FOR YOU - PART 2

Scarcity Is Not Real

The opposite of abundance is scarcity.

The essence of abundance is life-giving energy that is always creating more, ensuring that there is enough for everyone, always. The essence of scarcity is that life is in short supply, and we better grab what we can so we don't miss out.

The driving forces behind them are opposites, too. Trust perpetuates abundance. Fear ignites scarcity.

You can understand why it's easy to fall into scarcity. Whether it's about a diagnosis or finances or love or opportunities or friendships or success or wealth or winning or achieving; when faced with the fear of the possibility of not getting what you want or what you expected or what you think you're owed or what you believe you need, it can induce an almost panicked-frenzied-grab to get whatever you think will fill the gap.

Much of the world lives like it's the Boxing Day sales (or whatever the crazy retail sale weekend is in your country) every day, all day, where there is only a limited number of things available at a good price, so you must hustle and jostle and push and grab and sometimes even trample and steal and take to get the thing that you want.

Our governments do it to entire people groups, to whole ideologies, about all kinds of things. They store up and keep out and sanction to make sure they get what they think is theirs, what they think they are entitled to, leaving others in the dust.

But here's the thing: Scarcity is not real. It's a myth, a lie, a deception. Possibly the greatest one there is.

Alan Cohen said:
"The cause of poverty is not scarcity. It is fear and small thinking." (1.)

Fear drives scarcity, the mistreatment of others, the earth, and its resources. It is fear that walls up our hearts and homes and divides and subtracts. It's fear and terror that causes governments to behave inhumanly, prioritising wealth over human thriving. Fear is behind abuse and neglect and violence and tyranny.

What is it that we are so afraid of?

Dear one, there is enough, more than enough, to go around. Resources, food, water, kindness, education, transportation, dignity, knowledge, respect, healing, justice...

More.
Than.
Enough.

We are not in short supply of anything except perhaps the ability to see the abundance all around us; your sense of it within you.

(Caveat: this is not an excuse to use as much as we want in terms of the earth's finite resources. Being good stewards of resources is what ensures ongoing enough-ness for all.)

Time and again, throughout the scriptures, through our rich and beautiful and nuanced spiritual history, the Mothers and Fathers of our faith have told us through their stories and prayers and poems:

Do not be afraid.
Do not fear.
Have no fear.

It's not about eradicating fear, that's not possible. It's about not allowing fear the privilege of being the compass of our lives. Because when fear steers the way, scarcity marks the path.

Brené Brown said:
"After doing this work for the past twelve years and watching scarcity ride roughshod over our families, organisations, and communities, I'd say the one thing we have in common is that we're sick of feeling afraid. We want to dare greatly. We're tired of the national conversation centering on "What should we fear" and "Who should we blame?" We all want to be brave." (4.)

To go the way of abundance is brave and courageous. To breathe and take stock, rather than rush in and grab, takes discipline and control and a whole lot of trust.

I know, trust is hard. I know, your trust has been broken. I know, your trust has been pulled apart and trodden on, right in front of you.

And yet, trust lives on. And so do you. You carry on; you keep on going, you don't give up, there's more, there is enough. If your trust has been broken, healing awaits, wisdom is coming, this will not break you, it will make you.

The challenge is always and ever to keep on pressing into trust rather than fall back into fear.

Open up, don't close down.

Isn't that the message of faith? Isn't that what Jesus showed us? That even when all seems lost and gone and even impossible, it never is.

Abundance is not something you acquire; it is something you tune into. No matter where you are or what you're experiencing, or how you feel, or what's been taken from you, or what you feel is missing from your life, you can choose to flow into, harmonise, sync up with, the abundant life that is around you and within you, at all times, through it all.

Mindful Prompt: I choose to trust in the miracle of life, in the creative energy made by my trusting that there is more beyond this moment, beyond this broken trust, beyond this pain I'm feeling. I trust that I will rise again and heal and become and find my freedom.

THERE IS MORE FOR YOU - PART 3

You Are Never Just One Thing

Abundance is an 'and' word. The only thing it makes you choose between is whether or not you're in the flow of it.

In his book, from Good to Great, Jim Collins wrote extensively about the genius of the AND, and the tyranny of the OR. While Jim was writing mostly about business, the concept translates across all nooks and crannies of our lives, from our relationships to our work to how we see the world and whether we have any hope for tomorrow.

The tyranny of 'or' is the belief that you can only have one thing at one time.

You can be sad OR you can be happy.
You can be wealthy OR you can be ethical.
You can be spiritual OR you can be lost.
You can have time for your family OR you can have time for yourself.

You are good OR you are bad.
You are holy OR you are unholy.
You are a winner OR you are a loser.

'Or' is an 'in and out' kind of concept that rips you off and steals any hope of integration. It's a flow stopper. The tyranny of the 'or' forces you to believe that certain things cannot simultaneously live or be true, making your concept of the complex, beautiful and nuanced nature of reality into a two dimensional, diametric space where the pressure to choose the right way each and every time is paralysing.

Jesus told his friends and followers, who were under the rule and reign of a violent foreign military superpower, that he came to show them how to access and align with the abundant life that was available all around them, already, even in what they were going through. He said:

"I have come to give you everything in abundance, more than you expect—life in its fullness until you overflow." (5.)

Not bursting over with inconsequential just-enough-ness, but overflowing from stagnation to movement, from rigidity to flexibility, from stubbornness to openness,

From OR to AND.

Because, as you may have experienced, you can be:

Happy AND sad.
Ethical AND wealthy.
You can have answers AND you can still be learning.
You can have time for your family AND you can have time for yourself.
You can be spiritual AND be a little lost, too.
You can be good AND you can be bad simultaneously.
You can win AND you can lose.
When abundance is your MO, even a loss is a win because you learn and you grow and you become.
Losing is just as a good a teacher as winning is.

'And' is everywhere; it's in our sentences written and verbal a thousand times over. It's a little connective word that joins the dots on paper, in our hearts, in our minds, and in our lives.

Faith is not a full stop, it's a Divine 'AND' that makes space for our humanity AND our holiness, for miracles AND madness, for being lost AND found at the same time while still journeying on in a thousand different directions with different situations and issues in our lives in the many differing ways that we deal and process things.

You are never just one thing. You contain multitudes (Walt Whitman). You are an abundance of things, living in a world of abundance, generated from creative, divine energy - God, the source, the ground of being - who's essence is to flow into us at all times this abundance of life, of more than we could expect so that we overflow.

The idea of OR will have you believe that to have abundance, you need to leave where you are, experience different circumstances, acquire and attain or buy and collect different things.

But all you really need to do to experience abundance is open your heart to it.

Mindful Prompt: You are a living, breathing, manifestation of abundance. There is a multitude of things happening within you at any given moment. If all you can see is lack, look again, look within. You'll find it hidden within your skin.

LIKE ATTRACTS LIKE, WHAT YOU LOOK
FOR YOU'LL FIND, AND THE ENERGY
THAT YOU PUT OUT IS THE ENERGY
THAT WILL COME BACK TO YOU, TOO.

THERE IS MORE FOR YOU - PART 4
Abundance Is All Around

The world is an abundant place.

But what does that mean? What is that we have in abundance? Who gets to say who's version of abundance holds the balance of power? Depending on who you talk to, the answer to that question will be varied and different and contradictory.

It could seem that the world is abundant with hatred, violence, poverty, and oppression. It could seem that the world is abundant with tyranny and pain and war. It could seem that the world is abundant in struggles and strife. And at the same time, it could be that the earth is abundant with food and water and resources. It could be that our towns and homes and cities are abundant with helpers and dreamers and lovers. It could be that our countries are abundant in generosity and problem-solving and mercy and compassion. It seems as though there is an abundance of all things together at the same time.

The power of abundance is that it is whatever you believe it to be. It's a self-fulfilling prophecy. Like attracts like, what you look for you'll find, and the energy that you put out is the energy that will come back to you, too.

Before it was deemed a New Age concept, the Law of Attraction existed within Jewish belief and practice, and hence, within what is called early Christianity. The Talmud teaches that when you give generously to those in need, you get rich, and it promises that the more you give, the more you get. All throughout scripture, especially in the Old Testament, our Jewish Mothers and Fathers were taught as part of their fundamental value system, to take in strangers, to be kind to their enemies, to welcome the refugee and the orphan and the hungry, to give their best, not just their leftovers, to their guests, that hospitality can change and save lives, most of all, their own.

It's as Jesus said:
"Be wary of the shrewd advice that tells you how to get ahead in the world on your own. Giving, not getting, is the way. Generosity begets generosity. Stinginess impoverishes." (6.)

Stinginess is abundant with poverty.

Generosity is abundant with magnanimity.

You reap what you sow, like attracts like, what you look for, you'll find.

Rumi said:
"Wear gratitude like a cloak, and it will feed every corner of your life."

Mark Twain said:
"If you want love and abundance in your life, give it away."

Krista Tippett said:
"Our world is abundant with beauty and courage and grace."

Jesus said that he came to *"give you everything in abundance, more than you expect - life in its fullness until you overflow..."*

What is the world abundant with? What is overflowing in your life? What is it that you want? What do you believe about the earth and all that fills it?

I guess that's up to you.

Mindful Prompt: Consider what you believe about abundance, and whether or not you believe it about yourself. What would it feel like to believe that you are already in abundance? Practice that.

The Possibilities of Enough

The truth is, there is more than enough for everyone to share. A fundamental and generous essence of abundance underpins your existence. The founding Mothers and Fathers of our faith take it one step further and say that a fundamental and generous essence of abundance created and keeps on creating all that is in existence. Energy and matter are the overflow of Divine abundance. Creation can not help but be the result of God's generous nature.

In Judaism, part of the reason for creation and your being here is to be the recipient of God's goodness. In the creation poem recorded in Genesis, everything that was created embodied the goodness of the creator - a flow of generosity. The universe and all that pertains to it is predicated on the foundation of goodness, and the divine intention is to continue to provide goodness to all the realms of this world. God created the world as the supreme manifestation of good and sustains it by constantly offering to it the flow of goodness.

"I have come to give you everything in abundance, more than you expect—life in its fullness until you overflow." (7.)

Abundance is all around you.

I know it may not feel like it. It may feel as though there is so much lack in your life. Whether it be a lack of health and you're facing a mysterious chronic illness; or you're facing a devastating and life-changing diagnosis; perhaps you feel an acute lack in finances and resources; or perhaps you see lack the most when you look to those who lead our countries with their greedy and out of touch policies that benefit a few and hurt many; or maybe even still it's in your relationships - a lack of mercy and compassion and closeness, affection and touch and togetherness. Or maybe you feel abundance the least when it comes to what you believe about yourself.

It's hard to open yourself up to the possibility of abundance when what you lack is so glaring and visceral. But what if you did? What if you cracked your heart open just a little and took a second look from a different perspective? What if you saw your areas of lack as opportunities to experience wonder? What if you took your eyes off your lack for a few moments and instead looked at what you have in spades all around you? Maybe you need to move a little, change seats, look out a different window, walk the other way to work, let go of some fear, forgive some pain, whether it's self-inflicted or caused by another's hand.

Abundance has nothing to do with what you own, what your bank account says, where you live, and what you've achieved.

The natural state of the world, whether you can see it right now or not, IS abundance, enough-ness, connection, resources and energy and togetherness.

And we must rise up against scarcity and lack that tells us there is not enough and we are not deserving and we should take what's not ours and make it our own and we need to sure up our own ends at any cost so we aren't left wanting, because right now, we are so wanting.

There is more than enough.
And you are enough.
Abundant. Good. Resourceful.

Abundance got this whole thing started. Abundance keeps it going, and only abundance will take us into the future that we were created to experience.

Mindful Prompt: When you arise in the morning, think of what a miraculous privilege it is to be alive – to breathe, to think, to enjoy, to love. (Marcus Aurelius.) Gratitude opens the door to abundance.

A LOT CAN HAPPEN FROM A LITTLE.
AFTER ALL, THE ENTIRE UNIVERSE WAS
CREATED FROM A SINGLE SPARK.

Liz Milani

THERE IS MORE FOR YOU - PART 6
Belief is the Key

What do you believe?
Belief changes everything.

When you believe in lack - that it underpins your experiences and circumstances and situations; when you believe that lack is what you deserve, lack is all that you are good for, lack is who you are and where you are going; when you believe that scarcity runs the world and rules our countries and dictates how we live together; then lack is what you will get. It's all that you'll see. It's all that you'll touch. No matter how many miracles happen around you, and in you, if lack is your lens, it taints the colours you see.

That's why belief is crucial to your experience. And you get to choose what you believe.

You can believe that abundance is all around you, or you can believe that abundance is elusive.

It's hard work to change your mindset from scarcity to abundance. It's hard to look at your lack-lustre circumstances and believe that abundance is in there amongst it.

But what is your alternative?

The word for abundance in Ancient Hebrew is Shefa. It's more a name than a word because abundance is not so much an experience as it is a way of life and living and being. Shefa doesn't just mean 'having a lot' of something. Shefa is about openness and belief. In its highest form, Shefa is the Divine ongoing flow between creator and creation; the connection, life force, and energy between us.

Shefa is of two parts: giving and receiving. Shefa is always being given. Are you willing to receive it? Belief is all it takes to open yourself up to abundance. Belief is the key.

That's what Paul meant when he wrote to his friends and said:

"God can do anything, you know—far more than you could ever imagine or guess or request in your wildest dreams! He does it not by pushing us around but by working within us, his Spirit deeply and gently within us." (8.)

The Shefa is always being given, and we draw it into ourselves by actively receiving it. The idea is that if there is a true need for blessing, healing, and the manifestation of goodness in our lives, we have to seek it actively, we must be open to receiving it when it arrives. And this flow of giving and receiving and receiving and giving generates more and more, until its "more than you expect—life in its fullness until you overflow."

Do you believe your life is held together by abundance? Or do you believe that you're being torn apart by lack?

You get to choose your own adventure, even within the things that you don't get to choose like sickness and abandonment and trouble and heartache. You get to decide what you believe about yourself and your place in this world while these are happening to you. Make no mistake, each choice is hard. There is no easy belief. But that's ok, because you are full of courage and you can do hard things, and those hard things turn out to be the best things that bring you great joy.

Maybe you don't feel like you have enough of what it takes to believe or to do the work of gratitude, because it is indeed work. Changing your mindset is gruelling and takes guts (lucky you have guts, hey?!). But abundance can do a lot with a little. That's the nature of it. Give abundance an inch, and it will take a mile. That's the grace of it.

Mindful Prompt: A lot can happen from just a little. After all, the entire universe was created from a single spark. Abundance flows to you and from you, you just have to open your eyes and your heart to see that it does.

THERE IS MORE FOR YOU - PART 7
The Treasure Has Always Been Yours

There's a famous Chassidic story about a man, Isaac ben Yakil of Krakow, who dreams about buried treasure in a faraway place, and he travels there to find it. When he gets there, he doesn't find the treasure, but meets a guard who tells him that he had a similar dream about treasure buried under the stove of a man named Isaac ben Yakil of Krakow. Of course, Isaac ben Yakil goes back home and finds the treasure, which was in his own house the whole time.

Thus it is with abundance. At times, all that's missing is your perspective to see it.

Abundance is not about having more money or more resources or more time, or something more fulfilling and grand than you already have. Abundance is a way of being in the world; it's not something you acquire, but rather something you tune into.

Abundance is what happens when you stop needing more and start appreciating what you have.

Jesus, his friends, and his people were in desperate times under the rule and reign of a ruthless foreign military superpower who were stealing their lands, taxing them of nearly all their income, raping their women, murdering their children, and more. It was confusing, oppressive, and dark. Into this political and social atmosphere, Jesus said:

"I have come to give you everything in abundance, more than you expect—life in its fullness until you overflow." (9.)

And then, Jesus didn't lead them into victory against their foes; he didn't go all Robin Hood and steal from the Romans to give back to the Hebrews; he didn't plan a coup or encourage a resistance.

He died. Murdered. Executed by the people they were desperate to be free from.

It could seem that this abundance Jesus spoke of died with him if indeed it was about winning and achieving and dominating.

But that's not what abundance is about. It's about belief and gratitude and wonder. What do you believe about your life and the world, especially when things don't seem to be going your way? That changes everything.

There was an abundant source of life that Jesus was showing and teaching his friends how to access, even as they were slaves in their own homes and towns and lands.

Abundance isn't about acquiring and buying; it's about being and becoming.

It's about believing that there is more than enough to go around. If the entire universe lived in the flow of the power of Shefa (Divine Abundance), poverty would be eradicated, the sick would get the very best of care, our elders would not be hidden away as the end draws near, but would be celebrated and honoured for the life they've lived while they're still living it, our borders would be open, our doors would stay unlocked, our tables would be full, our arms would reach all the way around each other.

Abundance is ours for the believing. Abundance is yours for the choosing. And even if it takes a trip around the world only to discover that the treasure you were seeking was always yours, then I pray you find this abundance and let it flow, flow, flow your whole life long.

Mindful Prompt: What you seek is seeking you (Rumi), so let it find its way home.

"DON'T LOOK FOR MIRACLES. YOU YOURSELF ARE THE MIRACLE."

Henry Miller

YOU ARE THE MIRACLE - PART 1
Miracles Grow Slowly

The unfathomable, unbelievable, things you can't even imagine in your wildest dreams... Can you believe that these dwell within divine possibility?

Is a miracle only a miracle when it makes your life better?
Is a miracle only a miracle when it happens to Christians? People of faith?
Do miracles even happen?

When Ephesians 3:20 is quoted, the verses after it are usually skipped over to allow greater emphasis to fall on the words: *"more than you could ever imagine or guess or request in your wildest dreams!"* It brings to mind things like winning the lottery, instantaneous healings, people walking out of wheelchairs, bank accounts being filled like the twelve baskets of leftovers when Jesus turned five loaves and two fish into enough for a crowd of thousands to eat. Preachers and teachers encourage their crowds to have big hope and big dreams and believe for big impossible things because God can do *"more than you could ever imagine or guess or request in your wildest dreams!"*

And so people wait for God's magical lotto ball to drop from heaven making their lives miraculously, instantly better, while the rest of the verse goes unheard. It says:

"God does it not by pushing us around but by working within us, God's Spirit deeply and gently within us." (1.)

While people are raising their hands to the sky looking to pull down the goodness of heaven into their lives, God is waiting for them to notice what has already begun - the miracle happens within.

Unexpected, unbelievable, random, unexplainable, miraculous things happen all the time; in you, around you, through you, and through others. Can you believe?

Can you even believe the miracle happens inside of you, in your heart and spirit and body, as you travel through the unexpected highs and lows of life?

Can you believe that miracles dwell in the ordinary and everyday and normal things? When you embrace the random, unexpected things in your life with generosity, the good and the bad alike, you'll find miracles tucked into all kinds of corners in all kinds of places inside all kinds of people waiting for you to unfold them and see them for what they are.

The Divine does great things, things you can't even imagine, things beyond your wildest dreams, in people you could have never imagined, in situations you thought would be the end of you, in ways you could not have predicted.

Don't wait for the miracle to come to you; it's happening in you, through your perceptions and openness and willingness to see people and life and circumstances as the everyday ordinary miracles they are. They have come to you to set you free from 'waiting for the lotto ball of heaven to drop,' into a life where you draw continuously from a well of the miraculous within you to live the life you already have.

Despite popular opinion, miracles grow slowly. They come in human form, wearing skin, and breathing the same air that you do. They come to you wrapped in the ordinary moments of your life, hidden in the bizarre and the peculiar and the boring. Miracles are so because they're outside the realms of what you think is possible, expected, reasonable. God is already here. The miracle is already happening.

Mindful Prompt: What do you believe about miracles and your capacity for them? Your connection to them? The fact that you are one?

YOU ARE THE MIRACLE - PART 2

Everything is a Miracle

When you need a miracle, and it feels as though your life is dependent on the impossible becoming possible, to hear someone say that you and your life are already a miracle, can feel like a slap in the face.

When you're sick, and you need answers; when you have bills to pay, and you need provision; when you're in a bind, and you have no idea how you're going to figure it all out...

What you need is a miracle. Not some pseudo-guru who is telling you to open your eyes and heart and see that the trees and birds and grass and waves and children and all.of.life.around.you is a blinking miracle.

You need the antidote to your problem; the thing that is going to change it all around; give you space, a chance to breathe; wholeness, healing... peace. Things you don't currently have.

So, let's say you get your miracle. Let's say that your disease is healed; that money turns up on your doorstep or in your bank account, that a way was made for you to gracefully wade through the mess you found yourself in...

What happens the next time something comes your way?

Because it will. Life is full of the unexpected. Which is not all bad news; it's just the way it is. You will overcome and conquer, only to find yourself overcoming and conquering again. You finish old battles, only to find yourself in new ones.

Will you always wait for a miracle to bail you out?

Or will you discover that the miracle isn't so much in the instant healing, but in finding joy while you're struggling with illness; that the miracle is not in the instant providence as much as it is in the learning and resilience as you do hard things you didn't think you could do. Maybe the miracle isn't in getting what you need right now to bail you out of hardship, pain, and uncertainty, but instead, it's in your willingness to open your heart, even in this, and grow through it into something new, redeemed, wise.

This is how things *"work together for good"* (2). I know you've gone through hard times; everyone does. When you lean in and learn, the hard time can become the *'wound where the light enters you...'* (Rumi); the place where you found what you now have; where you began to understand what you now know; when you realised that healing or not, life is miraculous because that's the nature of it.

It's usually certainty that you're after when you're seeking specific miracles about specific things. When you haven't made peace with the fact that you can never really be sure, that life is one big lesson in the unexpected; when you've said all the faith words but haven't lived a faith life, certainty is the golden calf of belief.

Allow divinity to work deep within you, in the dark and hidden places, amid pain and trial and suffering. In this place of surrender, the miracle is that no matter what happens, you keep opening your heart to love, connection, joy, beauty, and wonder.

The unexpected has the power to unearth the miracles hidden within. The magic takes place when you open your eyes to God all around you, already in you, deeply woven into others, in the world, present, here, now.

Mindful Prompt: There are only two ways to live your life. One is as though nothing is a miracle. The other is as though everything is a miracle. (Einstein) How do you want to live?

YOU ARE THE MIRACLE - PART 3

For The Pure Joy Of It

Does your miracle need to be witnessed to be deemed one? Is it wasted if it happens in private, without the affirmation and praise of others? Is a sunrise less beautiful if no one sees it but the birds and the trees? Is a miracle still a miracle if all it does is make your face smile and your heart expand? Or does a miracle need to happen in a prayer line with anointing oil in a building while important people say important prayers?

Long ago, there was a wedding. A custom at weddings was that you served the most expensive, most delicious wine first, while everyone was sober enough to appreciate and enjoy it. Then, as the wedding progressed, and people drank more and more wine - less for the taste and more for the feel - you'd bring out the cheaper stuff. It has the same physical effect, but everyone's senses are dulled enough not to notice the drop in quality, and it saves the wedding host some cash. Which makes sense. Why waste the good wine on late-night frivolity when the cheap stuff will do?

But at this wedding, long ago, on a balmy Israeli evening, they ran out of wine altogether. Surely everyone had had enough; surely they didn't need any more. Surely they'd just make it work, run around town till they found something, anything, to serve the remaining guests and save not just the host's cash, but their honour, too (it was culturally shameful to run out of wine at weddings).

Mary asked Jesus to do something about it. And he did. Short story shorter, he took six jars that were used for ritual washing (think feet and hands), filled them with water, and turned that water into wine, as in, the very best wine you have ever tasted, and then they served it to people who were probably too drunk to notice. (3.)

Life is mostly made up of normal things - jars of clay filled with water to wash hands and feet. The miracle is that the Divine takes the fundamental things that we need in order to live, and transforms them into an elixir of joy - jars filled with the best wine you've ever had. Even at the end of the night when everyone is too drunk and spent to notice; when it doesn't really matter and doesn't seem to make any difference, the Divine puts on a show, just for you, just for the heck of it, the pure joy of it. God divinely brings together the natural and the supernatural, the pain and the joy, the suffering and the peace, the loss and the wisdom and brings heaven to earth right there in the middle of it all.

Miracles aren't about fixing and healing and making things better. Miracles are here for the pure joy of them. The pleasure of seeing the sunrise by yourself that does nothing but make your face smile and your heart expand is no less a miracle than water turning into wine.

Mindful Prompt: Keep your eyes and heart open. Miracles come dressed up as your ordinary, painful, joyful, everything in between, life. You never know when you'll experience the unexpected and witness a miracle in motion.

YOU ARE THE MIRACLE - PART 4

The Miracle Isn't Always In The Cure

Miracles come, too, through unexpected, horrific ways. Children rarely dream of being healed because children rarely dream that sickness and illness and lack and hardship will be a part of their lives. No one (hardly) expects to get sick.

But many unexpectedly do. Whether it's a physical or mental illness, a condition that visits every now and then or chronically sticks around, whether other people notice it or not, or it affects what you can do and how you move about in the world, or it's a result from an accident or incident, sickness settles in and changes the shape of your life.

And oh, how you long to be healed. To find the magic pill, the instant cure, that would change your life and make you, and your suffering loved ones, better.

You can read in the New Testament that Jesus healed many people - from leprosy to missing limbs to blindness and even from death - instantaneously. But he also walked past a great deal of them, too.

To be honest, I don't get it. Why he left some in their suffering, how he chose between who to heal and to leave. I don't get why some recover, and some don't. Why some seem to have lifelong battles with certain afflictions and others have cast iron minds and bodies.

There's a lot I don't know about sickness and healing and wholeness except that I do know this by experience:

The miracle isn't always in the cure.

That's where we WANT it to be. That's where we hope to find it.

But sometimes, often, and I'd even say, mostly, the miracle begins in the suffering.

Rilke wrote:
"So you must not be frightened, dear Mr. Kappus, if a sadness rises up before you larger than any you have ever seen; if a restiveness, like light and cloud-shadows, passes over your hands and over all you do. You must think that something is happening with you, that life has not

forgotten you, that it holds you in its hand; it will not let you fall. Why do you want to shut out of your life any agitation, any pain, any melancholy, since you really do not know what these states are working upon you? Why do you want to persecute yourself with the question whence all this may be coming and whither it is bound? Since you know that you are in the midst of transitions and wished for nothing so much as to change. If there is anything morbid in your processes, just remember that sickness is the means by which an organism frees itself of foreign matter; so one must just help it to be sick, to have its whole sickness and break out with it, for that is its progress. In you, dear Mr. Kappus, so much is now happening; you must be patient as a sick man and confident as a convalescent; for perhaps you are both. And more: you are the doctor too, who has to watch over himself. But there are in every illness many days when the doctor can do nothing but wait. And this it is that you, insofar as you are your own doctor, must now above all do." (4.)

The greater miracle while you're sick or struggling or suffering, is to wait, is to be with yourself in the struggle without catastrophising, without wishing you were somewhere different, endlessly googling symptoms and treatments and protocols, obsessing over whether you deserve it or not, brought it on yourself or not, the (un)fairness of it all, praying so fervently for deliverance, that you miss the miracle of life that is still present in your own.

Jesus healed many people, but being healed was something that happened to them. Their miracle was in having the courage to live the life they had before and after the healing happened.

Can you believe that life has not forgotten you, that it holds you in its hands; it will not let you fall? To find life amid an ailment is a miracle, but equally, so is the courage to find out who you are without it.

Mindful Prompt: Don't stop believing for a miracle, a cure, an end to what ails you. But know this: you do not have to wait for that to happen to experience one.

YOU ARE THE MIRACLE - PART 5
From Those You Least Expect

Sometimes, it's the people who carry miracles into your life that is the real miracle. Like when the neighbour you had written off, offers to pay for a new fence; the friend you thought was gone for good returns with an apology; the partner you thought would never forgive, shows faith in you; the person you can't stand turns out to be the only one there for you at the end of the day; the person you believe to be dangerous and harmful, whom you've been told is up to no good and is stealing the nations jobs and homes and welfare, turns out to be compassionate, kind, contributing, and just who you need for this season right now.

I wonder what miracles are missed because you overlook and dismiss the hands that hold them?

Before he was called Paul, his name was Saul, and he was the elite of his vocation. He rounded up followers of Jesus and enslaved them, threw them in prison, condemned them to death. He ran campaigns against the early church, was an enemy of the 'faith' in every way.

I bet no one expected him to become Paul. I bet no one could imagine that something would happen to him and he would return an advocate, friend, and teacher of the very faith that he had spent half his life trying to destroy. It's possible that many witnessed the executions sentenced by Saul, and then years later, saw Paul declare his love for Jesus and his commitment to 'faith.'

When you read that *"God can do anything... far more than you could ever imagine or guess or request in your wildest dreams..."* it's hard to imagine God doing miraculous things through people you can't imagine would ever have anything to do with God or miracles and your life.

What was the miracle of Paul? That he had a change of heart and became a new person and turned his life around? Or that people accepted him, and listened to him, and relied on his words and teachings to guide them in the faith that he had previously tried to extinguish?

Most of the people we hate are just people we don't understand. You will find that if you give it some time, a new perspective, and a little faith, the miracle would be that you would discover they are just like you. Worth a second chance, a second look, a little emotional generosity. Or at least, hopeful for those things, just like you are. And once your open our eyes and heart to them, you'll find the miracle of connection flowing between you.

Can you believe it?

Take a second, more divinely human look at the people you demonise, disagree with, write off, shut down, cross the street to avoid (you know I'm not talking about doing away with healthy boundaries), you might find something you don't expect, a miracle in the making, Saul becoming Paul... and who's to say which one of you is doing the changing.

All I know is that some of the most significant moments in my life came through people I would never have imagined.

Mary Oliver wrote:

"If someone you didn't know
told you this,
as I am telling you this,
would you believe it?

Belief isn't always easy.
But this much I have learned,
if not enough else—
to live with my eyes open.

I know what everyone wants
is a miracle.

This wasn't a miracle.
Unless, of course, kindness—
as now and again
some rare person has suggested—
is a miracle.
As surely it is." (5)

Mindful Prompt: Surely there are some miracles around you that you don't yet understand, but just as surely, you are on the journey to discovering them. All you need to have to find them is an open heart and mind.

YOU ARE THE MIRACLE - PART 6
The Possibility Of What Could Be

Miracles come when you least expect them, in ways you couldn't have imagined. They often come in the form of not getting what you want, of things going wrong, when things don't work out the way you needed them to.

In the days of the Bible, the Israelites had been waiting for hundreds of years - through oppression, violence, enslavement and trouble - for the Messiah to come and rescue and establish them as the head of the free world. They waited, worked, believed, and dwelt in the possibility of what could be.

And then, out of nowhere, God showed up. Not as a warrior or a general or a king, but as a baby birthed in a stranger's house, born out of wedlock, shrouded in scandal. Miracles can come through blood and pain and vulnerability, too.

Can you believe it?

Jesus grew from that small baby into a Rabbi and teacher. The hope of humanity didn't play according to the rules or expectations of those that had been hoping for his coming for centuries. He was betrayed by his own and murdered by a foreign military superpower. And after he rose from the dead, he disappeared into thin air without having overthrown the Roman Empire or freeing the Jewish people from its clutches.

There was no war; there was no humbling of Rome; there was no release from the shackles of enslavement.

The Saviour failed. Jesus wasn't the Messiah everyone expected him to be, prayed he would be, believed he should be.

And yet, the miracle came, became human, dwelt among humanity, declaring that the miracle isn't in having things the way you think they should be, but living fully and open-heartedly, doing what you can, while things are the way that they are. The miracle is hidden in the middle of your own life, not ensconced in a symbol or a person or even a religion, separate from yourself. The miracle is to be able to open your heart in the middle of the mess, surrender, and recognise what is right in front of you.

The miracle doesn't come in winning and conquering and proving, but in resilience and hope and love and connection.

Things don't happen the way you expect them to. That's life, right? I mean, if we could predict and guarantee what would happen with a reasonable level of certainty, things would be different the world over. But none of us can know what is going to happen. So while you expect and pray and believe and hope, stay open to the truth that miracles can happen in places and with people you never thought they could, which is part of the miracle itself.

You can be a victim of what happens to you, or you can be a miner of miracles, from the every day to the divine, no matter what happens.

Mindful Prompt: Sometimes not getting what you want is all the grace you need.

YOU ARE THE MIRACLE - PART 7
Allow The Unexpected To Happen

Can you believe that miracles come to you from all different people through unexpected events via unconventional means in ways you couldn't have imagined? Even through terrible and unexpected and unwanted experiences?

The miraculous thing about miracles is that you find them, they happen to you, in you, even because of you. While you're still mending, while you're still on the journey, in the middle of the fight, during the dark night of the soul, through people you'd rather not have anything to do with, miracles work their way into your life and become a part of who you are.

Paulo Coelho said:
"You have to take risks. You will only understand the miracle of life fully when you allow the unexpected to happen." (6.)

The more interesting question to ask yourself is not whether or not miracles happen, but whether or not you are open to receive the unexpected, whether or not you can surrender to what is knowing that something miraculous can come about even in it.

It's a risky way to live because it means you take down the walls around your heart, you stay vulnerable to the story of others, you commit to change and transformation, you remain present in your current reality, you cease (practice ceasing) numbing and hiding and avoiding... you open your eyes. Sometimes it will feel like you're opening your eyes in saltwater, other times, it will seem like the sky is clear, and you can see for days, and the pleasure of it could almost drop you to the floor.

Can you believe that even here, there is goodness, beauty, and wonder? Even in the middle of this? Even from this?

If you can't believe it, then I will believe it for you. It's almost the only thing I'm sure of: if you look for miracles, you'll find them. Not in the grand instantaneous spectacles peddled by prosperity healing preachers, but in the quiet, transformational, muck, mess, and marvellousness of your own life. In the opening of your own heart.

Henry Miller once said:
"Don't look for miracles. You yourself are the miracle."

And maybe that's it. You living open and free and true is more of a miracle than anything else.

Mindful Prompt: Instead of looking outward for miracles to come to you, turn your gaze inward. Imagine what miracles are already in you, a part of you, waiting to be birthed from your open heart.

"LET EVERYTHING HAPPEN
TO YOU. BEAUTY AND
TERROR. JUST KEEP GOING.
NO FEELING IS FINAL."

Rilke

ACCEPT AND ALLOW - PART 1
Work With It

In a letter he wrote to his friends in Philippi, Paul said:
"I've learned by now to be quite content whatever my circumstances. I'm just as happy with little as with much, with much as with little. I've found the recipe for being happy whether full or hungry, hands full or hands empty. Whatever I have, wherever I am, I can make it through anything in the One who makes me who I am." (1.)

Eckhart Tolle said:
"Accept - then act. Whatever the present moment contains, accept it as if you had chosen it. Always work with it, not against it. Make it your friend and ally, not your enemy. This will miraculously transform your whole life." (2.)

These two statements of the same kind are beautiful to read, but beyond that, the work gets challenging.

Paul learned how to be content. He learned. While he was in the middle of living his life, the things that happened to him taught him - through trial and error, success and failure, tragedy and joy - how to accept the present moment as if he had chosen it; content in all things, the good, the bad, the in-between.

Contentment seems like such an arbitrary, mediocre word. Children don't dream of contentment. They dream of the best of the best; of excitement and adventure and awe.

And yet... is there anything more needed? Anything more sought after? Anything more prized than inner peace come what may?

The acceptance of both bliss and tragedy is challenging.

People spend much of their lives doing everything they can to avoid suffering and heartache. They mask and pretend and hide and avoid and numb so as to not feel the pain. Because pain feels awful. And ironically, they do the same with joy and bliss and pleasure. Often when these things present themselves to people through their experiences and circumstances, they feel shame, undeserving and awkward. They don't quite know what to do with joy, so they ignore it altogether. Or, they abuse it and try to extrapolate joy and wonder and bliss and pleasure by force, wringing the life out of it.

You can learn how to be present and content to and with all the things that happen to you, the good, the bad, the in-between. It's about acceptance and freedom, the paradox of allowing pain a place in your life in order to set it free. It's about embracing joy even when many around you are suffering, and even when you feel like you don't deserve the wonder and bliss of pleasurable moments. You learn how to hold the paradox by sitting with whatever comes to you, rather than hiding, pushing, striving, pretending and ignoring.

Paul learned how to be content, how to be present, how to allow everything to happen to him, and still be at peace. He learned it. He went through it. He got through it.

And so can you. So *will* you.

Mindful Prompt: Accept, then act. Allow, then be free. And you too, like Paul, whatever you have, wherever you are, you can make it through anything in the One who makes you who you are.

ACCEPT AND ALLOW - PART 2

You Already Know The Secret

In a letter he wrote to his friends, Paul said that he had learned the secret to being content. The secret to accepting and allowing whatever came his way. Whether in plenty or in need, whether full or hungry, Paul learned that he could make it through anything by the power of oneness, through the One manifest in his own self, by being his own self. (3.)

God, The Divine, Ultimate Source, the Ground of Being - whatever name you call God - isn't on a mission to save you from yourself. The great salvation is to save you to yourself. The secret to being content, to be able to accept and allow pain and joy alike, to bear witness to the tragic and the blissful, to be present to and with your life, to be here now... is in you.

It's not out there somewhere. The secret is not something you have to journey outward to find; you must journey within. You must learn to sit with yourself and sit with all the things that happen to you. Allow them. Accept them. And even love them. Pain is just a messenger, joy is simply a gift. Give them a seat at the table and let them both work their unique miracles in your life.

Pain? Miracles? Really?

Yep.

The problem is, sometimes you're too busy avoiding all the things, to reap the benefits of all the things.

When you try to minimise pain with your behaviour through avoidance, you may experience short term relief. Still, you perpetuate and amplify long term suffering due to the pain itself and the things you do and use to minimise and numb it. When you fight pain, it actually triggers more pain, and what you end up avoiding is learning healthy ways to handle pain when it comes.

Sitting with it, whether it be pain, fear, anger, rage, joy, pleasure, love, change - whatever it is - simply means allowing it to be; resisting the urge to get rid of it, and not judging yourself for these emotions and experiences when they come.

It may seem counter-intuitive to allow so-called negative emotions space in your life, but that's only because the larger social and religious narratives have been to get rid of them and reduce them as quickly as you can without too much fuss. Pain is often misunderstood to be weakness. But it's not. It's a messenger that has vital information, and even gifts, to share with whom it visits. People spend too much time avoiding the very things that would grow, heal, and free them.

Allowing can seem scary to a person of faith when much of faith has been about dis-allowing, protecting, judging, hemming in, prohibition, and renunciations. But allowing is exactly what needs to happen. Acceptance of what is, is the only way forward. The only way for your broken leg to heal is to allow it to be a broken leg so that you can get the help it needs to fuse back together and grow strong again. Your broken leg is what's happening to you, to pretend and ignore and fight and cast out and demand and judge will only make it worse and delay your healing.

You will not lose your salvation (what a concept!) by allowing the hard things a seat at the table of your life alongside the good things. You will not disappoint God if you embrace your suffering. You will not shame the Divine by enjoying pleasure and basking in joy. You are not opening your life up to any kind of evil or damage or disgrace or slippery slope by accepting what is happening to you, what has come to you, what is in you.

Paul learned to be content in it all. He embraced it all within himself. He found peace, not by wishing things away, but by living them all the way through.

Mindful Prompt: "Whatever the present moment contains, accept it as if you had chosen it. Always work with it, not against it." (Eckhart Tolle). This is the real work. This is the miracle - that you would choose your life, rather than run from it.

ACCEPT AND ALLOW - PART 3

Pain Is A Messenger

Pain is hard because it's painful. We'd much rather avoid it altogether. So we numb and avoid and judge and hide and pretend. We try to push our pain away. The only problem is, we end up pushing our pain onto others instead. If you do not transform your pain, you will most assuredly transmit it - usually onto those closest to you: your family, neighbours, co-workers, and, invariably, the most vulnerable around you.

Pain comes to us in many forms: tragedy and loss, physical and mental, accidental and abusive. Running from it, avoiding it, numbing it, pretending it's not there, is not going to ease it for you.

Pain is the physical sensations or signals telling you that something is happening within your body in relation to an event or situation. Suffering is the story you tell yourself about the pain. Pain is unavoidable. Suffering is (mostly) optional. Suffering is what happens when you can't (won't) face what's happening here and now. You have 'this' but what you want 'that.'

You minimise suffering by accepting pain. Acceptance is not approval. Acceptance is not resignation. Acceptance is not wallowing. Acceptance is allowing what is to be what is.

What else can you do with this moment than let it be what it is? Can you see how people spend so much time and energy trying to make the present moment anything other than what it is?

Pain is a messenger, it's a signal, an alarm system, for your body and heart. So pay attention. Accept it. Allow it. Don't run or hide or numb.

Give it a seat at the table, pour it some tea, let it speak. Give it space to tell you its message. If you stay long enough, you'll hear the voice of God in it.

You don't heal pain by punishing it. You love your way to health. When someone you love (or even just like only a little bit) is in pain, you don't treat them with animosity or disdain or as if they have failed. More often than not, the first thing you do when someone you love is in pain is reach out and touch them, embrace them, hold their hand, offer them your support. Why is it so different when it comes to your own pain?

Wounds that are loved become wisdom that heals.

The Psalmist said:
"Is there any place I can go to avoid your Spirit? To be out of your sight? If I climb to the sky, you're there! If I go underground, you're there! If I flew on morning's wings to the far western horizon, you'd find me in a minute - you're already there waiting! Then I said to myself, "Oh, God even sees me in the dark! At night I'm immersed in the light!" It's a fact: darkness isn't dark to you; night and day, darkness and light, they're all the same to you." (4.)

God is with you in the sky-high moments and the ones where you feel buried underground.

Sitting with pain doesn't mean you resign yourself to a life of it. It doesn't mean that you're giving up - quite the opposite. To sit with pain means that you're ready to hear, to learn, and then to act. Remember - first, we accept, then we act.

Elizabeth Gilbert said:
"[Pain] is one of the most powerful energy forces in the universe—but only if you use it as an instrument of change. People must be willing to journey all the way to the bottom of their pain and experience full catharsis—to completely break apart so they can then rebuild themselves anew. As Jim said, "Suffering without catharsis is nothing but wasted pain." The world is filled with people who have suffered horribly and crawled away broken. They never reached catharsis; they just got shattered and stayed shattered. And then there are the great masters (Gandhi, Mandela, King) who used their suffering as an incredible engine to transform into something better." (5.)

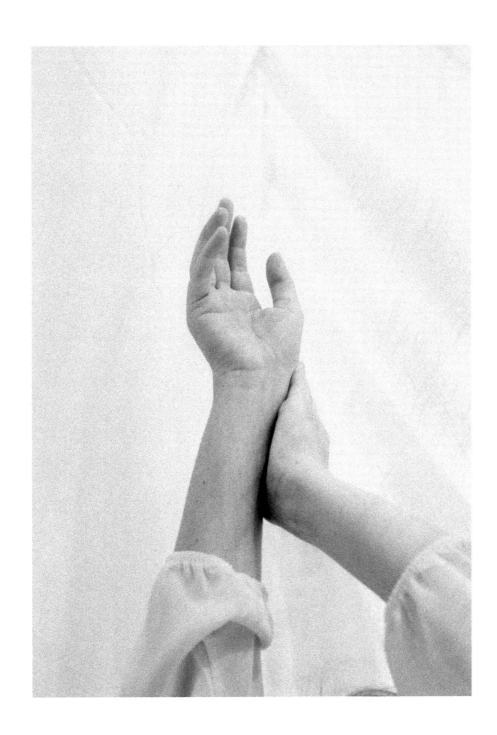

Mindful Prompt: Pain doesn't have to break you. That's not its purpose. It can, miraculously, end up rebuilding you. Sit with your pain and let it spark in you the transformation that moves you through it and beyond

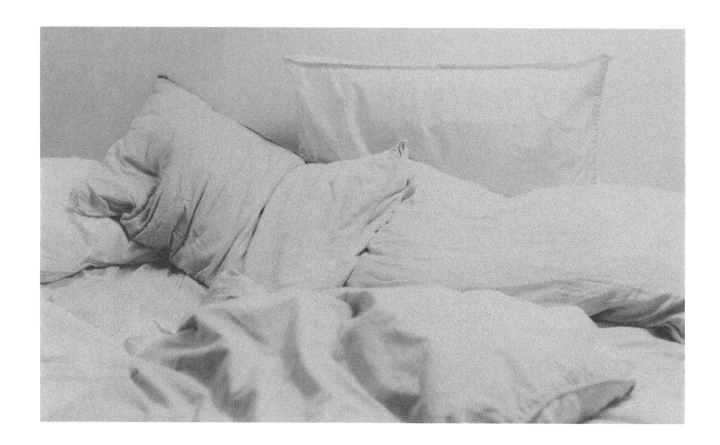

ACCEPT AND ALLOW - PART 4

Enjoy The Joy

Pleasure is not sinful.
Joy is not a luxury.
Bliss does not belong to another faith tradition
heretical to your own.
Wonder is not only for creatives and children.

Allow yourself to enjoy the joy.

Joy and happiness is nothing to feel guilty about or
be ashamed of. I'm not sure why some won't allow
themselves to experience pleasure, and even delight
in it when it appears in their lives. Maybe due to an
austere sense of faith and service, joy has been seen as a
frivolous venture, not serious enough for the dedicated

and committed. Perhaps in the misunderstanding of
the scripture *"the joy of the Lord is your strength,"* some
seek joy outside of themselves. And maybe for all our
empathy and sensitivity, we wonder how on earth we
can allow ourselves to enjoy even the little things when
many people around us don't even have little things to
enjoy.

Here's what I know:

There is more than one chair pulled up to the table of
your life. You can have empathy for refugees, and put
your hands and feet to justice, while at the same time,
allowing yourself to enjoy the pleasures that come into

your life. You can experience both compassion for your neighbour who has a terminal disease and wonder at the beauty of the ocean, at the same time. You can sit with the joy of your children and the frustration of an unjust health care system at the same time. You can be serious about your faith (whatever that means) while enjoying a movie, or a novel, or dinner with friends, at the same time.

Joy is not a luxury. Pleasure is a necessity. You cannot get through your life healthily without allowing yourself to revel deeply in whatever joy you can find, or that finds you. It's your holy responsibility to find joy and let it have its way with you.

Some say that *"The joy of the lord that is [your] strength..."* (6), as if God's joy is something found outside of your body and personal experiences; holy joy instead of other kinds of joy. But there is only joy and your experience of it.

Theologian and scientist Teilhard De Chardin said: *"Joy is the infallible sign of the presence of God."*

And that joy? It's not high and mighty and unattainable. It's earthy and salty and sweaty and messy and pure. It's as simple as this: where there's joy, God is there right in the middle of it.

You were created to experience happiness and pleasure in your heart and in your body. You have a holy responsibility to allow yourself to function the way you were created. It is not sinful, wasteful, or indulgent. Joy is how you save your own life; experiencing it with others, is how you save theirs.

Mindful Prompt: Sit with your joy. It's not something you have to work for, deserve, buy, or prove. You can only accept it, allow it, and then, of course, enjoy it.

How often do you have nothing to do? Nothing to think about? Nowhere to go, no list to complete, nothing urgent that needs to happen as soon as you can make it happen?

Nothing doesn't seem to happen for anyone too often. There is always work to do, family to attend to, errands to run, shows to watch, music to listen to, podcasts to binge, children to raise, friends to catch up with, obligations to be fulfilled, fun to be had, kids sport to endure, exercise to push through... there are endless amounts of things to fill days, eyes, mouths, ears, hearts, and minds with the world over.

But nothing?

Shouldn't we always be doing something? I know that value doesn't lie in productivity, but does anyone actually live like they believe that?

When was the last time you stopped and sat with nothing. Nothing to do, no problems to solve, nothing to watch, no one to talk to, no phone in hand... just you and your body and your soul?

Nothing is something you should accept and allow, and often. Although the world values and prizes productivity and being busy, more and more we are discovering the sickness of a life that has no margin in it, no room for stillness. Whenever you're running at a hundred miles an hour, you might be able to ignore the mess, but at some point, you will come to a stop, either on your own volition or forced via circumstances, and you won't be able to pretend it's not there. Not if you want to heal. Not if you want to rebuild your strength.

Accept nothing. Allow it space in your life. Fight to have moments, days, seasons of nothingness.

ACCEPT AND ALLOW - PART 5

The Holiness Of Nothing

You might start a meditation practice. You might call it prayer. You might just call it taking ten minutes for yourself, or you might just stare out the window for a bit (one of my faves). But do it. Let yourself rest.

Because as it turns out, your value does not lie in your productivity. Not even a little bit. Besides, you'll only be able to contribute as much as your times of rest give you strength for. You might as well accept nothing into your life, allow it room, and let it stay a while.

Rumi said:
"The quieter you become, the more you can hear."

Eckhart Tolle said:
"Wisdom comes with the ability to be still. Just look and just listen. No more is needed. Being still, looking, and listening activates the non-conceptual intelligence within you. Let stillness direct your words and actions." (7.)

It's in this stillness you find within, in your moments of nothingness, where you find that "peace that surpasses understanding" that Paul talked about in one of his letters (8).

Nothing is something that you have to fight for. You have to make a choice to put aside all the things that want your attention and your energy. Work towards stillness. Accept it and allow it. Let nothing wrap you up in its arms as it digs out that deep well of peace within you.

Mindful Prompt: What is your relationship like with nothingness? Do you live as though your value is connected to your productivity? How can you accept and allow moments of nothing into your life?

ACCEPT AND ALLOW 6

Work With What You've Got

There is perhaps no more despairing of an emotion than disappointment. Anger hurts, pain is hard, fear is debilitating, but disappointment?

It's crushing.

Being disappointed, and being a disappointment, are equally horrifying. And the kicker is, it can seem like life is strung together by a series of them. Things and people and seasons and hopes and dreams don't turn out the way you wanted them to, hoped they would, needed them to. And sometimes, neither do you.

Life lets us down, and we let life down. It's something that we can't foresee with the bright-eyed wonder of our childhood years - we start off with great expectations of ourselves and others and life, and bit by bit we discover the limitations of it all.

And it's so disappointing.

That's ok. The work is to allow and accept it.

Don't run from it, or numb it, or ignore it. Don't fill the space up with things and stuff and plans and ideas and lists and more and more and more in an attempt to drown out the disappointment because you don't know what else to do with it. That won't work. It will still be there no matter how much you try to bury it.

Accept the fact that life is not without its limitations.

I think that's the biggest thing: to acknowledge disappointment is to acknowledge limitations, both our own, and that of others, and even of God.

Honestly, God has disappointed me. Or perhaps, my concepts and ideas about God have led me to a disappointing theology and practice.

Accept it. Allow it. When you do this, you'll realise that it's not the worst thing. When you do this, you'll be able to move on.

When you face limitations and disappointments, both of your own doing and of others, you'll discover the reality of your situation. And from here, you'll discover that you can work with what you've got. And from here, you'll discover that realising your limitations and experiencing disappointment is a step in the journey of faith that will lead you somewhere good.

Paulo Coelho said:
"When you find your path, you must not be afraid... You need to have sufficient courage to make mistakes. Disappointment, defeat, and despair are the tools God uses to show us the way." (9.)

The Psalmist said:
"If your heart is broken, you'll find God right there; if you're kicked in the gut, he'll help you catch your breath." (10.)

Disappointment is soul-crushing. But the Divine? God is close during the breaking. God is present in it and to it. Divinity isn't scared of it, doesn't hide from it, nor pretends that it is anything other than what it is. So why should we?

Don't run from your own broken heart, love it back to life.

Disappointment is no less of a holy moment than joy.

Mindful Prompt: Disappointments are normal and natural and nothing to be ashamed of. It's all part of it, and it all belongs. The more you accept and allow this, the more you will have to work with moving forward.

ACCEPT AND ALLOW - PART 7

Let Everything Happen To You

Paul wrote to his friends and said:
"I don't have a sense of needing anything personally. I've learned by now to be quite content whatever my circumstances. I'm just as happy with little as with much, with much as with little. I've found the recipe for being happy whether full or hungry, hands full or hands empty. Whatever I have, wherever I am, I can make it through anything in the One who makes me who I am."
(11.)

Fast forward a few verses, and he finished his letter by saying:
"Receive and experience the amazing grace of the Master, Jesus Christ, deep, deep within yourselves." (12.)

The grace of contentment isn't something you'll achieve or buy or earn. It's only found deep, deep within yourself.

Contentment grows not as your circumstances improve, but as you show up to your own life, moment by moment, as it is, in full acceptance of now.

It's no easy feat and takes a lifetime to master. It takes courage and discipline to show up in all your vulnerability and compassion for pain, heartache and disappointment. And it takes just as much effort, work, and grit to show up for pleasure and joy and wonder, too. Thankfully, contentment, learning to accept and allow whatever comes your way without hiding, numbing, ignoring, or pretending, is something you can practice. Life will give you many opportunities to learn.

Rilke said:
"Let everything happen to you. Beauty and terror. Just keep going. No feeling is final."

Whether you have much or little, whether full or hungry, hands full or hands empty. Whatever you have, wherever you are, you can make it through anything in the One who makes you who you are (thanks, Paul.)

Show up. Accept and allow your life as it is. Stare it full in the face. No feeling is final. Nothing is permanent. Everything is moving. As you accept and allow it, you give it permission to work its way through you, and then finally, beyond you.

Cheryl Strayed said:
"How wild it was, to let it be." (13.)

Faith, at its most authentic, will lead you straight to the heart of your own life and self; that deep, deep place within where grace has been seeded, and it's silently, beautifully, blooming. Faith doesn't rush or hurry or get too busy to show up to 'here and now' for what it is. Faith has the courage to let it be in order to let it go. Faith is wild like that.

Mindful Prompt: Accept, then act. Allow, then be free. And we too, whatever we have, wherever we are - we can make it through anything in the One who makes us who we are.

"LOSE YOUR MIND, COME TO YOUR SENSES."

Fritz Perls

COME TO YOUR SENSES - PART 1

Faith Is A Full Body Experience

Come to your senses. Wake up. See things as they are. Feel your way to the holy centre of things.

This phrase is generally used to convey a sense of reason and logic. It's the idea that there is a common sense; that together as a community or culture we agree that some things and practices and ideas make sense - they are collectively reasonable and logical - and others don't.

How do you decide what makes sense and what doesn't? Is it just a 'feeling,' a sense that something is or isn't right? Do you rely on your senses? All of them? Or just a couple at a time? Do we taste, touch, see, hear, and smell our way to an agreed place of understanding that something is sound and good and right or otherwise?

Paul wrote to his friends and said:
"Come back to your senses and awaken to what is right." (1.)

In the Message translation, the above scripture reads:
"Think straight. Awaken to the holiness of life." (2.)

How do you wake up? What do you wake up to? A life divided where some things are holy, and other things are not, and you hope and pray and work and strive to be on the holy side of things?

Fritz Perls said:
"Lose your mind and come to your senses."

Your whole body is involved in determining what you think is reasonable, true, holy, real, or not. It's a full-body and spirit experience. In our modern, western culture, we are divorced almost completely from our physical senses. We rely heavily on our intellect, without realising that our body - everything we see, touch, taste, smell, and hear - is already involved in our understanding of reason. We tend to think our way out of what our body is saying, we deny it its voice and allow our thinking-mind to take us away from the present moment, and all that is in it for us to experience with our whole body.

Seeing and hearing and touching and tasting and smelling all tell vital parts of a single story. Common sense can be arrived at not from a consensus of our peers or culture or community, but the common agreement shared by the receptors in our bodies. Sometimes you need to stop thinking and let your body speak.

For the Ancient spiritual Mothers and Fathers, Christianity and belief was a multi-sensory experience.

That's why our faith tradition (including Judaism and most faith traditions in existence) is rich with rituals involving all the physical senses, and more than just the five we usually think of.

Scientists, philosophers, and psychologists alike believe there are up to thirty-three senses. We have the original five, and then there are things such as our sense of balance, space, pain, memory, and intuition.

Your body and spirit are sensory powerhouses designed to wake you up to the holiness of life; designed to sense the Divine in every aspect of your life.

Come to your senses. Show up to them. Give them the floor and let them speak.

Mindful Prompt: Pick one or two senses. With them in mind, bring your attention to your breath, in and out, in and out. Come to one of your chosen senses like it was a dear friend, a teacher, a loving parent. Pay attention to it. What is it telling you?

COME TO YOUR SENSES - PART 2

Deep Like The Ocean

Some of us have had the 'sense' taught right out of us. We don't know how to trust our bodies - sight, touch, taste, sound, and smell, and intuition, and pain, and heart. We're afraid of what we may come across if we let our physical senses interact with our spiritual nature. Maybe you've been taught that the human *"heart is deceitful above all things, and desperately wicked; Who can know it?"* (3.) The Message Bibles says: *"The heart is hopelessly dark and deceitful, a puzzle that no one can figure out."* (4.) It seems to be a foundational pillar in many modern faith circles that there is nothing fundamentally good about you at all.

The word used for deceitful in the verse above is 'aqov.' It comes from the root word we get the name Jacob from, which means "to grab the heel." Because of the Old Testament character of Jacob, we think that this word automatically means "to deceive," and most biblical translations use that word. But 'aqov' just means heel. The Septuagint (which is the earliest Greek translation of the Hebrew Old Testament completed around the 2nd Century), used the word 'bathuno' when translating 'aqov.' Rather than meaning something wilfully deceptive, it is the idea of depth, things that may seem hidden because they run deep. It was often the word used to describe the deep sea.

Our early Church Mothers and Fathers took the word 'aqov' and translated it, not to the idea of deception, but deep knowledge that we cannot comprehend, that we have to dig out, that might even lean more toward intuition. There's something in the story of Jacob that has been lost in lazy translation. If you look at the verse in context, it makes sense that "the heart is 'deep' above all things" - it runs deep, it has great depth - especially when you pair it with its outro, "who can know it?"

The Ancient Hebrew word for 'desperately wicked,' means nothing of the sort. It's the word "anesh" and it means "mankind in a state of weakness and helplessness." The word we would use for it today is

Vulnerable.

It's not that your heart is evil and deceitful and desperately wicked. Your heart runs deep like the ocean, an endless exploration of sense and knowledge

and memory and feeling. Your heart is beautifully, and often tragically, vulnerable, at the mercy of life and those you share the world with. Your heart is a sensory playground/minefield. You feel, you experience, you go deep. That's how you were made to be.

This verse is not about not trusting yourself. It's about what to do with the experiences and stories your body speaks to you about.

Thomas Merton said:
"At the center of our being is a point of nothingness which is untouched by sin and by illusion, a point of pure truth, a point or spark which belongs entirely to God... This little point of nothingness and of absolute poverty is the pure glory of God in us." (5.)

Come to your senses.

The rest of that passage in Jeremiah says:
"But I, God, search the heart and examine the mind. I get to the heart of the human. I get to the root of things. I treat them as they really are, not as they pretend to be."

The deception happens when you leave your senses out of the equation; when you don't include them. The way to find out who you are, what you believe, and what you should do, is to go deep, go within, find that point of pure truth that's connected to all of you, body, soul and spirit.

If you feel like a deep-sea of experience and emotion, and you feel like you've lost the connection between your body and your spirit, don't run for the shore! Dive beneath the waves. As Thomas Merton said, that's where God is. Eternity stitched into the heart of every single one of us. It comes from within, not without.

Mindful Prompt: Forgive yourself for believing that you are wicked, and embrace the truth of who you really are: human, holy, flawed, worthy, graced. Every time you feel that old controlling and manipulating deception of apparent wickedness, just hold those words in your mind and heart until it drowns out all other noise.

COME TO YOUR SENSES - PART 3
Divinely Natural

The body doesn't lie.

It will tell you when it's in pain; when it's heard a scream or a laugh; when something is wrong; when things are right; when danger is near; when beauty is before you. Your senses are designed to communicate all kinds of things. Since humanity has been able to feel and be conscious of its feeling, we have relied on our senses to keep us alive and thriving.

Until now.

We've forgotten how to hear. We don't know how to read our own bodies. We numb our souls and our senses with adrenaline and substances and TV and shopping and all kinds of things. As a society, we've switched the senses off. Of course, we still see and hear and touch and taste and smell... but as Jesus asked time and time again:

"Are your hearts still hard? You have good eyes, yet you still don't see? And you have good ears, yet you still don't hear? Neither do you remember?" (6.)

It's no wonder we don't trust our senses when our hearts are so hard we've forgotten how to feel them.

What is it that your eyes long to see and your ears itch to hear and your nose twitches to smell and your hands burn to feel and your mouth waters to taste?

We're so conditioned by fast food and fast faith and fast love, and pacifying, and gratuity and greed and angst... we're so keen to numb our pain and confusion - and the flip slide, our beauty! Cos what the heck do we do with that?! - that what we reach for with our senses is nothing that digs deep, that satiates and nourishes.

What if you could trust your senses? What if you could taste and see that God is good? What if you could hear the Divine in the still small whisper on the side of the mountain? What if you could feel the scars in Jesus hands and feet like Thomas did? What if you could smell the perfume of the woman who washed Jesus feet with her tears and hair? What if you could see the Divine in the other? In your enemy? In your neighbour? In yourself? What if Christ really is the way, and the truth, and the life? And that the Christ exists in us, among us, stitched into the fabric of things?

Come to your senses.

In his book, The Healing of Creation, John Philip Newell said:
"Christ is often referred to in the Celtic tradition as the truly natural one. He comes not to make us more than natural or somehow other than natural but to make us truly natural. He comes to restore us to the original root of our being. As the twentieth-century French mystic-scientist Teilhard de Chardin says much later in the Celtic world, grace is "the seed of resurrection" sown in our nature. It is given not to make us something other than ourselves but to make us radically ourselves. Grace is given not to implant in us a foreign wisdom but to make us alive to the wisdom that was born with us in our mother's womb. Grace is given not to lead us into another identity but to reconnect us to the beauty of our deepest identity. And grace is given not that we might find some exterior source of strength but that we might be established again in the deep inner security of our being and in learning to lose ourselves in love for one another to truly find ourselves." (7.)

Mindful Prompt: Do you trust your senses? Maybe you need to rebuild your narrative around your body and your natural response to the world to one of grace.

COME TO YOUR SENSES- PART 4

Skin In The Game

How do you know what's Godly and what's not? How do you know what is right and true and holy? How do you discern the senses? Of yours and others? What about when you disagree with someone? What about when your teachers and mentors disagree with each other? Who's right and who's wrong?

Since its creation, the Biblical Text in all its forms and translations has been used to support all kinds of injustices, from slavery to infanticide, to the oppression of women and more. As we've learned to wrestle with the text and see it as it was written - culture and context and medium and narrative - we've relearned some of these passages and have changed our interpretation of them. In fact, that's how it was designed to function in the first place - that we would always be learning and re-learning, constructing, deconstructing, and reconstructing what we think we know and believe.

How do you - YOU - discern what is right and wrong? If the Bible isn't clear, can you rely on the words on its pages? Can your body and spirit get involved?

It's not one way or the other; it's a communal effort.

Have you ever wondered why you are quick to draw a line? Good and evil? A list of do's and don'ts?

Dualistic thinking is good for our ego. It compares good people to bad people, in which we almost always determine ourselves and our motives and interpretations to be good. It determines who's in and who's out. It's very clear and blunt and decided. It makes us feel certain and safe.

But, when you get up close and personal to people and situations and life and even yourself, it's not that easy to draw the line. Good and bad are often hard to separate. Jesus dealt with lives, not lines. Discernment is a spiritual practice of listening, not a list of rules and regulations.

Henri Nouwen said:
"Discernment is a life of listening to a deeper sound and marching to a different beat, a life in which we become all ears."

Discernment is a full-body experience, it's multi-sensory. To discern something, you need to get your skin in the game. You need to get up close and listen with your whole body and heart and Spirit.

Don't be trapped by dualism. Instead, fight to remain open-hearted to the idea that everything belongs; that some things are good AND bad; that things aren't as clear as they seem. It's the challenge to stay open to Spirit and life. It's a humility that says, "I have more to learn; I'm not done yet."

Discernment takes the practice of paying attention to nuance and taking your time to feel your way to the holy heart of it all. Because that's what the heart of it all is - holy. No matter what you find when you come to the root of things, it's a sacred arrival.

True transformation is birthed in openness, not constriction. Discernment doesn't close things down with a judgement or a definition; it opens things up to be heard and felt and seen and known. Discernment takes all of your senses.

Mindful Prompt: Consider how your senses have helped you make decisions in the past, how they guide you here and now, and how they can continue to do so in the future.

COME TO YOUR SENSES - PART 5
Finding The Holy Hidden Truth

What does your body do when you're feeling different emotions, or when you're in certain situations? How does it react and respond? Does it tense or loosen? When you raise your voice, do your muscles tighten, too? When you breathe deep, do you feel your body relax? When you get good news, or bad news, or an angry text or DM, or when you fail or succeed... have you ever noticed that your body reacts, too?

Your senses pick up on everything.

Listening to your senses and engaging your body will give you clues and insights about how an incident, or behaviour, or situation, has impacted you, and even more, whether or not you should continue down the path that you're on.

Come to your senses.

That's the beauty of Thomas's story as told in the Gospels. The poor guy gets such a bad rap for wanting to engage his senses in the resurrection of Jesus.

That's the beauty of the woman who'd had her period nonstop for twelve years, and how she just needed to touch Jesus, feel something different, and have that sensation flow back through her body.

That's the beauty of the five loaves and two fish turning into a feast that fed thousands. And not just any feast, but a miraculous, political protest of class and economics and gathering... where you could hear and taste and see and touch and smell what Jesus had done.

That's the beauty of the blind man whom Jesus healed, whose eyes were opened.

That's the beauty of Jesus' weird and wonderful parables - those who have ears, let them engage their sense of hearing. Not just hear the words, but as Henri Nouwen said, the "**deeper sound... a life in which we become all ears.**"

I'm not saying that every feeling we get is truth, if it feels right, do it. I am saying that every feeling has a message, and if you follow it all the way, you'll come to the truth of it.

If you feel like you need a bottle of wine every night, then yes, that feeling is most likely one that you shouldn't listen to... on the surface. Beneath the desire for a bottle of wine every night is a deeper, more true story being told about what you're trying to numb with that bottle.

Perhaps what you really want is peace. Or rest. Or that you don't want to face your situation, that you're feeling overwhelmed, that things are a little hard right now.

And those feelings? They straight up need to be valued and heard and seen and listened to. They will lead you to the holy hidden truth of your heart.

Glennon Doyle said:
"A surface desire is one that conflicts with our Knowing. We must ask of our surface desires: What is the desire beneath this desire? Is it rest? Is it peace? Our deep desires are wise, true, beautiful, and things we can grant ourselves without abandoning our Knowing (our sense of what is holy and true). Following our deep desire always returns us to integrity. If your desire feels wrong to you: Go deeper. You can trust yourself. You just have to get low enough." (8.)

Come to your senses. Follow them into the deep, true places within you.

Mindful Prompt: Pay attention to your body, take note of how it feels when different things happen to you, when different words and emotions are experienced, and consider how your body's reaction is leading you to truth.

WE MUST ASK OF OUR SURFACE DESIRES: WHAT IS
THE DESIRE BENEATH THIS DESIRE? IS IT REST? IS IT
PEACE? OUR DEEP DESIRES ARE WISE, TRUE, BEAUTIFUL,
AND THINGS WE CAN GRANT OURSELVES WITHOUT
ABANDONING OUR KNOWING " - GLENNON DOYLE

COME TO YOUR SENSES - PART 6

The True and False Self

Through scriptures such as:

"I have been crucified with Christ, and I no longer live, but Christ lives in me." (9.)

and

"For if you choose self-sacrifice and lose your lives for my glory, you will continually discover true life. But if you choose to keep your lives for yourselves, you will forfeit what you try to keep." (10.)

and

"Trust in the Lord with all your heart and lean not on your own understanding." (11.)

we've concluded that our bodies are not spiritual; that our belief in God is the only good thing about us; that who we are deep inside, body and soul, is unholy and unworthy and wicked and no good can come from us at all.

We've turned body and spirit into a duality of entities; divorced, and at odds.

Paul wrote to his friends in Galatia and said:
"For the flesh desires what is contrary to the Spirit, and the Spirit, what is contrary to the flesh." (12.)

And the powers that be decided that when Paul used the word 'flesh' he meant our bodies, our 'selves,' our actual flesh and blood lives, and from that, it's been taught that to gain a spiritual life, we have to deny our physical one.

When you read on from that verse, you find clues about what Paul meant. He went on to talk about acts of the 'flesh' and then fruit of the 'spirit.' Paul was trying to communicate the tension between the False Self, and the True Self... the scripture could read: "For the EGO desires what is contrary to Truth..."

True self and false self are terms introduced into psychoanalysis by D. W. Winnicott in the '60s. Dr Winnicott used the term 'True Self' to describe a sense of self-based, spontaneous, authentic experience - a sense of "all-out personal aliveness," or "feeling real".

The 'False Self' is a defensive mechanism designed to protect the 'True Self' by hiding it. Dr Winnicott suggested that when in health, the False Self was what allowed one to present a polite and mannered attitude in public. But he saw more serious emotional problems in patients who seemed unable to feel spontaneous, alive, or real to themselves anywhere, in any part of their lives, yet managed to put on a successful show of being real. These people suffered inwardly from a sense of being empty, disconnected, or feeling fake.

Richard Rohr said:
"Your True Self is who you are and always have been in God. At its core, your True Self is love. Love is both who you are and who you are still becoming, like a sunflower seed that becomes its own sunflower. Most of human history has referred to the True Self as your 'soul' or 'your participation in the eternal life of God.' Too much of both religion and common therapy seem to be committed to making people comfortable with the 'False self.' It's just rearranging the deck chairs on the Titanic, which is going to sink anyway. To be rebuilt from the bottom up, you must start with the very ground of your being. The spiritual path should be about helping you learn where your true ground, your deepest truth, and your eternal life really are. Our common phrase for that is "finding your soul. And the discovery of our own soul is frankly what we are here for.

Your soul is who you are in God and who God is in you. We do not 'make' or 'create' our souls. We only awaken them, allow them, and live out of their deepest messages."

Come to your senses. What are they telling you about who you are at the very ground of your being?

It's not body OR spirit, but rather, body AND spirit. Your flesh and blood is just as spiritual as your heart and soul.

Mindful Prompt: Are you able to identify some of the ways your false self protects your true self by hiding it with things like projecting an image, or holding a standard? Give yourself permission to journey on to that true self deep within you.

COME TO YOUR SENSES - PART 7

Feel Your Way There

Come to your senses.

Be present with your eyes and ears and nose and hands and feet and skin and feeling and sensation.

Your body and spirit are not at odds with each other. You don't have to deny your physicality - your senses and desires and instinct and intuition - to embrace the spiritual journey. Your body and spirit make a great team. They point to each other. They cannot exist apart from the other.

Paul wrote:
"My old identity has been co-crucified with Messiah and no longer lives; for the nails of his cross crucified me with him. And now the essence of this new life is no longer mine, for the Anointed One lives his life through me—we live in union as one! My new life is empowered by the faith of the Son of God who loves me so much that he gave himself for me, and dispenses his life into mine!" (13.)

Your 'self' - body, soul, and spirit - and the Divine are joined: "we live in union as one." Together, communal, integrated.

God is in YOU. The Divine speaks to you THROUGH your body. Your feelings, your sensations - touch, sight, sound, taste and feeling; and the other senses like balance, memory, and pain - tell a story about what is going on in you and around you. When you're self-absorbed (operating in the false self), you'll interpret your senses in such a way that you'll want to build even more walls around your heart, becoming even more absorbed in your protection, safety, and certainty. But when you're self-aware? You'll come to your senses, and they will lead you to truth, grace, connection, and love. 'Self-aware' and 'Spirit-aware' go hand in hand. I would even go so far as to say that they are one and the same.

Paul also said:
"Think straight. Awaken to the holiness of life." (14.)

That's what your senses are designed to do; wake you up to the holiness all around you, in you, and the

holiness happening through you. Every sight and sound and taste and tactile energy is a force of wakefulness. Do not turn them off. Do not become desensitised to your own body and feeling. Your senses are vital; you need them to help you stay awake to who you really are and what is really important.

St. Catherine of Sienna said:
"Be who you were created to be, and you will set the world on fire."

Being yourself is the continual practice of shedding all the layers of projection and image, looking good, wanting to be liked, being scared to stand out, and trying to be who you think people want you to be. Being yourself means being naked, raw and vulnerable. Being yourself means owning your senses and letting them lead to the holy hidden heart of you.

You are allowed to feel your way to holiness just as much as you are allowed to believe your way there.

Maybe you need to lose your mind (let go of the false self that wants to continually hide, project, divide and separate; that wants to protect and build walls around your heart) to come to your senses (your true self that senses the Divine within, and without; your spirit in union with Christ).

Your body and your heart and your mind are not a source of evil. They are a source of connection and communication. They are intrinsically involved in your experience of love and life and grace and faith. God loves your whole self, maybe it's about time you did, too?

And that includes the failures and the disconnections and the confusion. It all belongs. It all adds up. It's all holy.

Eckhart Tolle said:
"There have been many people for whom limitations, failure, loss, or pain in whatever form turned out to be their greatest teacher. It taught them to let go of

false self-images and superficial ego-dictated goals and desires. It gave them depth, humility and compassion. It made them more real." (15.)

Come to your senses. All of them. They have something holy to tell you, to show you, to lead you to. Wake up to the holiness of life. Show up to everything that you feel in your body. Honour it. It will give you more depth, humility, and compassion. It will make you more real.

Mindful Prompt: Sit comfortably. Close your eyes. Breathe into your belly. As you breathe out, make a sound. Be with that sense of breath and sound. Feel the sensation of air flowing over your lips, down your chest and deep into your stomach. Allow the feelings of this simple act of honouring the life force within you to wake you, revealing the holiness of this moment, even here, even now.

"WHEN I STAND BEFORE
THEE AT THE DAY'S END,
THOU SHALT SEE MY SCARS
AND KNOW THAT I HAD MY
WOUNDS AND ALSO MY
HEALING."

Rabindranath Tagore

YOU WILL HEAL FROM THIS - PART 1

Healing Is Not A Reward

Healing, it turns out, isn't about some whiz-bang, instantaneous occurrence where heaven and earth collide, and sparks fly, and in a single moment, something that was one way, becomes another, better, whole, back to the way it was always supposed to be, free from affliction and pain and separation. Healed. Whole. Done.

Preachers say, "Your healing is signed, sealed, and delivered by the blood of Jesus!" Whatever that means, and however that works, those words don't inspire the same hope that they used to for many.

For many who have prayed and cried and believed and wished and hoped and have been good and nice and sacrificial and proper and upright, healing hasn't come. Maybe that's you. Maybe you've believed hard, but your healing is still beyond the horizon, a seemingly vast distance away. A youth pastor I once knew used to say: "If you have faith and do not doubt, whatever you ask for in Jesus name will be yours, yes and amen," as if it were a magic spell, a formula, a spiritual hack to get the healing that you are convinced you need to live a meaningful life of vitality and joy.

Maybe some people have experienced an instantaneous moment of relief, healing, release, where their heart or body, or whatever was ailing them, became well in a single conscious moment. Although I have not experienced it, I have heard others tell their stories about it.

We are led to believe that the instant healing from what ails us in our bodies, minds, hearts, relationships, and more, will make our lives better, grander, more fulfilling, beautiful, and, ultimately,

Worthy.

Healing has become a trophy of the blessed, something that happens to the "called out ones, the chosen, the holy and righteous and good ones," as if there are groups of those who are, and groups of those who are not. The first thing most people think about when they are diagnosed, or receive traumatic news, or discover some horrific thing that dramatically affects their life, is:

What did I do to deserve this?

Let me tell you, here and now, friend, the Capital T Truth that I stake my life on:

What ails you has nothing to do with your worth, value, or what you deserve. And your healing doesn't, either.

If you want to heal, you must put to rest your scales of worth and value. You must lay down your measuring stick of success and meaning. There is no such thing as the perfect condition with which to live your life. There is only the life you have and the will you have to live it here and now.

Healing happens as you allow yourself to mend from the damage that ridiculous standards of perfection and wholeness and purity have set upon you; that a good life means a pain-free life. That an able life is a body without difference, without breaks, without scars.

Dear one, I pray that you heal from believing you have to be anything other than what and who you are, in your heart and body and mind, to live this life that is yours, full, and deep, and true, and holy.

Mindful Prompt: Do you need to deconstruct some of your beliefs about healing, what it is, and how it happens? Start here, in a moment of prayer and meditation. Close your eyes, follow your breath, picture the word 'healing' and take note of what feelings and sensations arise in your spirit, heart, and body as you do. Healing is not a reward or even a gift. It is a path you walk; it is what you were made to do.

THERE IS NO SUCH THING AS THE PERFECT
CONDITION WITH WHICH TO LIVE YOUR LIFE.
THERE IS ONLY THE LIFE YOU HAVE AND THE WILL
YOU HAVE TO LIVE IT HERE AND NOW, AND BEYOND.

YOU WILL HEAL FROM THIS - PART 2
The Radical Acceptance Of What Is

Being healed is not going to heal you.

There is no healing for the human condition. You cannot eradicate pain and fear and suffering and worry from your life-experience. You just can't. You will heal from this ailment, only to find another somewhere down the track that you will need to heal from again. You may find a solution for your propensity for anxiety, but what will you do when something worse happens, and it comes back with reinforcements?

Perhaps what you need to be healed from most is the idea that your life will be better, more meaningful; that you can do better and be more successful; that you will feel God more fully and be able to serve others more purely, on the other side of whatever it is that is ailing you.

Healing is so much more than having your broken leg instantly put back together after being prayed for at the church's altar. Healing is so much more than your broken heart being mended during a single prayer session at a bible study. Healing is so much more than your illness being found gone and your doctors' bewilderment after you've fasted and called down fire from heaven around your friend's dinner table. I'm not mocking these things. I know they are very serious. But I am saying these things are not The Thing.

Healing happens not when, but as, you continue: AS you keep on living, AS you keep on opening your heart. Healing happens when you stop distracting yourself with thoughts and prayers of miracles, and you live the miracle, this one wild and precious life that you have, like nothing can stop you. Healing happens as you run towards your ailment, not with thoughts and prayers of condemnation and frustration, but with open arms and love and grace.

Healing begins with the radical acceptance of what is. Acceptance and resignation are two different things. Acceptance says: this is what I have to work with; this is what will get me to the next thing. Resignation says: I am stuck here in this, with this, and I'll never be able to move on.

Accept, don't resign. It won't always be like this. And things won't ever go back to being the way they were. The miracle is that this will not ruin you, it will make you, it will heal you, it will build within your life and body and heart, the gracious resilience that life wants for you so that you can show up with love and purpose no matter what, no matter when.

Paul told us that it's by transforming our minds that we change our lives and the world. (1.) Not miracles or instantaneous unexplainable healings, but the process and lived experience of transforming over time, through whatever it is you are in. What do you believe about yourself and the world and your body and your neighbour and others and how we all fit together and belong to each other? Not what you say you believe, but what you actually believe, which you can figure out by observing your actions, thoughts, and decisions.

Belief doesn't have to be true to behave so. Sometimes the biggest healing you can receive is the willingness to change your mind. Often, being able to change is a bigger miracle than anything else.

Mindful Prompt: Although it might not feel like it, you are not at your limit. You are vast; you contain multitudes. You are stronger than you think and more capable than you know. To discover that this is the truth, all you have to do is believe it.

YOU WILL HEAL FROM THIS - PART 3
Face Your Wounds

It is said that Jesus rose from the dead with healing in his wings, and for many, they have taken that to mean that somehow, while Jesus was dead, he acquired the power to heal. Yes, he healed people around him while he was physically here on earth, but now? All one needs to do to capture the healing they need is to pray and believe, or to get someone more anointed and holy then they, to pray and believe. And this healing? That Jesus dripped in when he rose from the dead? Can be ours (note the subtle hint of sarcasm).

Jesus didn't rise with healing in his wings. Firstly, he didn't rise with wings. He rose as the human he was when he was executed, except for one thing: his scars. The King of Glory, Saviour of the universe, the one who was and is and is to come (remember that old adage?), who was (is) all-powerful and mighty, defeated death, rose from the grave,

and kept his scars?

You would think that the ultimate healing would include the erasure of the hurt and the pain and the affliction! That the wounds that brought death would be obliterated, to be remembered no more, conquered, pure, gone.

No.

Jesus kept his scars.

You don't heal by running away; by putting as much distance as you can between yourself and whatever has ailed you, whether it be physical, spiritual, matters of the heart, or what is more likely, a messy mixture of it all.

You heal by facing your wounds, by embracing your trauma, by taking your illness in your hands and gazing into its eyes. You heal by going all the way into your wounds. This is how transcendence begins.

When Jesus was executed by a foreign military superpower as a terrorist and a usurper of the peace, maybe part of what the whole story has been trying to show us is this principle of going in, not running away. He went all the way into death. He drew it in close, held it, faced it, owned it, even, became it. Jesus held death in his body, his heart, his spirit, and he healed from it. He showed us what it is to enter into the cave we fear, to find the treasure we seek (Joseph Campbell). Jesus didn't obliterate death, he transcendent it - he showed us what it is to face the things we think we cannot endure, and come out the other side, healed, whole, scarred, beautiful.

Scars are not things to be ashamed of. We prize the smooth, unblemished skin of babies; how soft and clean and pure it is, while we shame ageing skin, covered in the tattoos of the life we've lived. But it's all a prize. Scars aren't signs of your weakness, but of your ability to heal. They tell the story about how the wound that was once there, that bled and hurt and screamed and bruised, eventually, with care and love and grace, came back together and healed.

Not back to the way it used to be... we don't heal to become who we were. We heal to become something new.

These days, the death, burial, and resurrection of Jesus means more to me than a ticket to heaven. Jesus' lived experience shows us what it is to enter into trauma, feel the pain, face it, find forgiveness, let it go, and rise, rise, rise, like a glorious phoenix from the ashes, into something healed and whole and new.

Mindful Prompt: You can never go back. Even though I know sometimes you wish you could, and you long for days gone by, I promise you: tomorrow will come, and today there is grace for you to be here, to find beauty, to face your fears, and to continue on, until you find the joy you thought you left way back in the days you long for.

SCARS AREN'T SIGNS OF YOUR WEAKNESS, BUT OF
YOUR ABILITY TO HEAL. THEY TELL THE STORY ABOUT
HOW THE WOUND THAT WAS ONCE THERE, THAT BLED
AND HURT AND SCREAMED AND BRUISED, EVENTUALLY,
WITH CARE AND LOVE AND GRACE, CAME BACK
TOGETHER AND HEALED

"IF YOU DESIRE HEALING,
LET YOURSELF FALL ILL"
— RUMI

YOU WILL HEAL FROM THIS - PART 4
Breakout With Your Sickness

You don't heal back to the way you were before, to who you used to be. When your body heals, it doesn't revert back to its old state. Maybe there will be scars, or new shapes and feelings and colours and movement. You heal into something new, something beyond where you once were. Still you, but you becoming you, too. God always said God would make everything new (2), and healing is how newness manifests itself in the world.

We must embrace our ailments - our illnesses and pain and damage and heartbreak and wounding - pull them in close, even welcome them when they come, because it's through them that we heal and become and are made whole.

Think of it as an immune system. Very simplistically, for an immune system to become strong - to become itself in the sense of being able to do what it needs to do to protect us - it needs to get sick and recover, get sick and recover, get sick and recover.

Rilke said:
"Why do you want to shut out of your life any agitation, any pain, any melancholy, since you really do not know what these states are working upon you? Why do you want to persecute yourself with the question whence all this may be coming and whither it is bound? Since you know that you are in the midst of transitions and wished for nothing so much as to change. If there is anything morbid in your processes, just remember that sickness is the means by which an organism frees itself of foreign matter; so one must just help it to be sick, to have its whole sickness and break out with it, for that is its progress." (3.)

Rumi said:
"If you desire healing, let yourself fall ill."

This is not giving up. This is surrender. Surrender is not giving into whoever and whatever. Surrender is how you enter into flow. It's how you work with what you've got. It's how you accept yourself and where you are and what you have and what you don't and you forget about trying to control the things you can't and you move forward with the things that are yours to

steward.

Surrender is scary because the fear of what happens after we surrender, after we let ourselves fall ill, after we break out with our sickness and give it space to do what it needs to, is real. What if I don't get better? What if things get worse? And perhaps the biggest fear of all:

What if I'm not strong enough to handle this?

Surrender, my love. Flow. Breathe. And like breath, let whatever is happening to you and around you flow through your life; inhale, exhale. In, out. Here, and gone again.

You can face your trauma, your pain, your fear. You can face this mess that you're in, the nothingness that you feel, the mountain you have yet to climb. You can face it. It won't kill you. You will not be swallowed by grief and darkness and pain and worry. You will not drown or burn or be overcome to the point of being finished. Facing your life is how you begin to heal, not how you begin to lose. When you run from your trauma (or whatever is you don't want to face), it will chase you down your whole life long in one way or another, and you will try to hide from it in so many different, destructive and numbing ways, only to feel it lurking right behind you, licking at your heels. You think your damage is a lion, driven to devour you, ready to feast upon your weakened heart. But it's not. It's like a small child, crying, unable to see through the tears and fear, confused and flailing. It's chasing you not to get you, but because it needs to be held and loved and known and made to feel safe by you.

Stop. Turn around. Open your arms. This is your healing. Not your destruction.

Mindful Prompt: "Perhaps all the dragons in our lives are princesses who are only waiting to see us act, just once, with beauty and courage. Perhaps everything that frightens us is, in its deepest essence, something helpless that wants our love." Rilke.

YOU WILL HEAL FROM THIS - PART 5

You Don't Need A Fresh Start

Healing is your true nature.

There's a perception that we start off perfect - baby smooth and innocent, unblemished and unbroken; a blank canvas ready to be painted upon by a life yet to be lived - and progressively descend into corruption. The aim of the game is to break and bend and descend as little as possible. Don't stuff it up. When you talk about the possibility of having a fresh start, what you mean is that you want to go back to that place of perfection, almost a place of 'nothingness' - blank space upon which to re-paint your life anew.

You don't need to start again. You don't need a fresh

start. You only need to surrender to what you were created to do:

Heal.

Mark Nepo said:
"We often move away from pain, which is helpful only before being hurt. Once in pain, it seems the only way out is through. Like someone falling off a boat, struggling to stay above the water only makes things worse. We must accept we are there and settle enough so we can be carried by the deep. The willingness to do this is the genesis of faith, the giving over to currents larger than us. Even fallen leaves float in lakes, demonstrating how surrender

can hold us up." (4.)

That is more along the lines of what the Apostle Paul was trying to convey when he said that God said to him:

"My grace is enough; it's all you need. My strength comes into its own in your weakness." (5.)

Whatever it is that needs healing in your life right now, don't move away from it. Don't curse it, or run from it, or blame it, or use it as an excuse to close your life and heart down to the possibilities that still exist for you, even though you are certain there may not be many left. Settle. Breathe. Be still. Allow yourself to be carried by the deep. This is grace. Not that you would be removed from the process of discovering how you can heal, but that you would be brought right into the middle holy magic of it. The miracle is where you are. Not out there somewhere with someone else with other things back when you were perfect and clean and un-lived.

Here. Now. As you are. With what you have. Sick. Broken. Scared. Tired. Unsure.

Miracles dwell in the mess, even mess such as this. Give over to the current running through you that is larger than you. Look to the leaves, see how they float, let them tell you how surrender holds them up, and carries them to new shores.

Mindful Prompt: You might feel like you're about to fall off the boat, or that you're struggling to swim, maybe even to breathe, as you reach around you for something to hold onto, to get you out of the water. But this water is not going to drown you. Its intention has always been to carry you. Stop your striving. Still yourself. Give over to the current beneath you. Surrender. Grace will carry you on.

Soothing As A Spiritual Practice

Allow yourself to rest. Give yourself permission to engage in restorative activities, even if they include little activity. Comfort and soothing is a spiritual practice, not an indulgence.

Condemnation never healed anyone, so why, dear one, do you think it helps to condemn yourself because of the challenges you face?

When you're ill, or experiencing lack, or are travelling through failure, or are broken-hearted; when you're ailed in any way or form, it's easy to believe limiting things about yourself and to speak to yourself in a diminishing way. But let me tell you, and I know these things for sure, you are not:

A failure.
A burden.
A hopeless case.
Done.
Finished.
Broken.
Dirty.
Sullied.
Used up.
Insignificant.
Beyond repair.

When Jesus looked over a crowd of people experiencing a myriad of heartbreaking things, living in one of the most volatile political and social times in history, oppressed beyond what you could imagine, he didn't weigh up whether they were worthy, he didn't test them to see if they were capable, he didn't care whether they came by boat or by plane or by foot or however, he didn't make a quick judgement based on bias and opinion and contribution versus cost—none of that.

Jesus looked upon his friends and fellow country-humans, and a feeling welled up inside of him that moved him to action:

Compassion. (6.)

God lives in you. The Christ energy, Spirit, the power that rose Jesus from the dead, is stitched into your being, in your cells and spirit and blood and breath. It's longing for you to see yourself as Christ does, and to show yourself the same energy that Spirit pulses all around you and in you with:

Compassion.

Self-compassion, care, comfort... this is how you heal.

This isn't just an abstract idea; self-compassion is something practical you can do for yourself. Self-soothing is a spiritual practice. And look, it's not about pseudo-self-care, as in, I'm going to eat the chocolate and watch the Netflix. Self-soothing are things that you can do to calm your body, your nervous system, and your spirit down in the effort of compassion and making yourself feel safe and at home.

Things you can do to self soothe could be things like deep breathing, prayers and mantras and blessings, meditation and music, being in an environment that makes you feel warm and safe, like a bath or a favourite blanket or candlelight. Think of the things you would do for a child to make it feel safe; the times that you felt safe when you were a child.

When your body and heart and spirit are experiencing dis-ease and fracture, it can be a disorientating. In a sense, you almost become like a child again, looking for comfort and safety and reassurance; to find that feeling of being held and safe.

You can do that for yourself.

Love yourself well, and you will love yourself well.

Mindful Prompt: When you're tempted to face whatever it is that is ailing you with judgement and fear, and things that make you feel less than and unsafe, take a moment to look at yourself through the eyes of someone who loves you. Allow compassion to rise up within you for yourself. You are not a burden or a failure or a lost cause. You are a miracle in motion. Give yourself what you need.

YOU WILL HEAL FROM THIS - PART 7
Healed And Still Healing

You will heal from this.

I know you want to, and if you choose it, I know you can, and I know you will.

Obviously, I cannot know the outcome of your physical illness. I cannot know, nor can I guarantee, that your relationship will mend. I cannot promise you that the things you're experiencing in your life will culminate the way you want them to.

And that's ok, because that's not what healing is, anyway.

Miracles are not what you think they are. They are not (only) people getting out of wheelchairs and the blind being able to see and cancer shrivelling and diseases retreating and anxiety vanishing and afflictions leaving. I long for the day, and I think we are on our way, when we believe that people with differing abilities and experiences are seen to live full and happy and miraculous lives.

You know what a miracle really is? Being here. Showing up. Owning yourself. Taking responsibility. Letting the love you have for yourself influence how you love others. Empathy. Compassion.

Compassion is a radical miracle that would change the world if we healed all the things within us that want to condemn ourselves and others. Or at least, embarked on the healing journey.

Because this is true, too. You are healed and healing at the same time. There will always be some kind of tension in your life, because you cannot heal yourself from the human condition. In fact, you're not meant to be healed from the human condition, but from the belief and idea that you need to be anything but

human to experience life and love and grace in all its miraculous fullness.

You will heal from this. You will heal from all the ways hatred cuts you to pieces, and how shame makes you hide, and how heartbreak twists you up, and injustices make you feel murderous, and how abuse makes you feel used up and worthless, and how failure makes you feel wrong, and how your anger and outbursts and the way you hurt the people you love makes you feel like you're creating more damage than doing anything worthwhile...

And all the other things... you will heal. This is your holy, human work. Participate in your healing, and you'll participate in the healing of the world. Healing is of one piece. It's a global tapestry, and we are all threads within it.

Healing is not a reward, or even a gift. It is a path you walk; it is what you were made to do.

Rabindranath Tagore said:
"When I stand before thee at the day's end, thou shalt see my scars and know that I had my wounds and also my healing."

When you stand at day's end, having lived and loved and shown up through it all, your scars won't tell the stories of your failures and weakness and trouble. They will declare, loudly and with grace, the stories of your healings, of your miracles big and small and in-between. Of how you rose, and rose again, and continued on, and healed and kept on healing.

Mindful Prompt: Dear one, I pray that you heal from believing you have to be anything other than what and who you are, in your heart and body and mind, to live this life that is yours, full, and deep, and true, and holy.

"THE ACHE FOR HOME LIVES IN
ALL OF US, THE SAFE PLACE
WHERE WE CAN GO AS WE ARE
AND NOT BE QUESTIONED."

Maya Angelou

SAFETY FIRST - PART 1
The Illusion Of Control

What does safety mean for you?

Images of walls and fences and fortified interiors with doors and locks and gates and curtains and comforts; spaces where nothing can come in or get out without thorough checks and balances and expressed permission, quickly come to mind. As humans, we crave safety for ourselves and our loved ones. It's one of our basic survival needs. It's hard-wired into parents and lovers and brothers and sisters and friends. More than half of the average income goes towards creating and keeping safety in the form of shelter and transport and insurance and food and medical and devices and so many other things. We go to extraordinary lengths to have a sense of safety, and somehow keep it in play.

We even go to war in the name of safety.

There's a certain sense of safety found in control: controlled environments, emotions, places, and situations. If you ask yourself about a time where you felt less safe, I wonder if it was also a time when you felt you had less control over a situation?

Control gives you a false sense of security.

Why false? Because control is an illusion. It's a narrative, and we really want it to be true. But time and time again, we discover ways in which we have no control. It doesn't matter how many walls you build, how carefully you curate an experience, how much insurance you have physically and/or metaphorically, life always gets through the cracks and upsets controls equilibrium.

The writer of Ecclesiastes explained this when they wrote:

"In my pointless life, I've seen everything - from the righteous person perishing in his uprightness to the wicked one who lives a long life and keeps on doing wrong." (1.)

In other words, there are no guarantees, no matter how hard you try, or not.

There is wisdom in housing and food and keeping your children safe and buying insurance and making good choices about your body and health and safety. I hope you have a safe place for your heart to land, and a safe someone to share your life with, and a safe place to get a decent nights sleep. Safety is something that everyone should be entitled to. Being safe should not be the privilege that it is.

Maya Angelou said:

"The ache for home lives in all of us, the safe place where we can go as we are and not be questioned."

I think that's what we really want. And in our pursuit of it, we mistake safety for control. Mostly, what we're trying to control is the comfort of our bodies and hearts, because we have been tricked into believing that safety happens wherever comfort does.

There are two kinds of safety.

There is one that is a measured, regulated, and managed space, where everything is in its place, and it's monitored and watched, and there's data and control and outcomes and wishful predictability. Comfort. Low risk.

Don't risk living a life in order to be safe, comfortable, measured, acceptable.

There is another kind of safety that doesn't feel safe at all. It's the safety of belonging. It's found in authenticity, courage, and faith. You discover it when you risk it all to be who you really are. It's the safety you find when you are true to yourself. You are only as safe as you are true.

This is the kind of safety the Psalmist talked about when they said:
"In peace I will both lie down and sleep; For you alone, O Lord, make me dwell in safety." (2.)

Mindful Prompt: What, where and who makes you feel safe? Take a moment to consider what these things and people are keeping you safe from. Is this safety keeping you small? Or helping you become more whole and more you.

SAFETY FIRST - PART 2

Safe In The Most Unsafe Way

How do you keep your heart safe, practically speaking? What do you actually do to protect your heart and body from everything that comes against it?

Do you fence it in, wall it up, monitor access?
Do you play it safe in life and love and expectation and dreams and hopes?
Do you measure everything, temper your desire and longing?
Do you keep the truth inside of you, smothering it with acceptable answers?
Do you deny and isolate, numb and ignore?
Do you hold it all in?

If you desire to keep your heart from breaking, you've come to the wrong life. You are not unbreakable. No one is. I know that seems like the worst news in the world, but it's not.

When you dig into the Psalms and the Proverbs that talk about how God is your strength and your refuge, a safe place for you to land, you realise that the person who wrote it did so as a lament. They were grieving. In other words, their heart was already broken.

During hard and difficult times, individually, communally, and globally, people often say that the only place they are safe, is in God - God is the only place/entity/thing that keeps them safe.

How does that work?
How does God do that?
Is that what God is for?

Your reflex, or conditioning, to protect yourself is, as my friend Nicole Sachs says, keeping you safe in the most unsafe ways. It's a kind of safety that keeps you small, isolated, untrue, and folded up. It restricts and constrains. It prefers lies that keep the peace and saves face and makes other people comfortable at the expense of the truth. But don't forget what truth does...

It makes you free.

True safety is found on the other side of letting go of the small life. It feels risky and uncertain. It feels like everything other than safe. But that's just your ego getting in the way, wanting to stay in control, wanting to keep you small so that you can stay comfortable.

Living with your heart wide open makes you vulnerable to heartbreak. It makes you vulnerable to the pain and suffering in the world. It makes you vulnerable to negativity and abuse and cynicism. But it also opens you up to joy and experience and trust and faith. It makes you vulnerable before love and grace and hope.

How else do you think God keeps you safe? Do you think the Divine hides you away from the troubles of this life? Making you immune and unbreakable and small and hard like concrete?

The spiritual path, the divine life, opens you up so wide that as your heart breaks, and it inevitably will, and encounters suffering, and you experience pain, you discover resilience and compassion and forgiveness and strength. Because that is where you are truly safe. Not when you hide, but when you learn that you can face it all, and thrive.

In this place, you'll finally feel the grace you've been searching for. It's in the great expanse of your life, waiting for you to do the safest thing for your heart and soul that you can do: put them in the game, where they were designed to be, and let them live, let them be what they are. Be who you are. That's where you're most safe.

Brené Brown said:
"Embracing our vulnerabilities is risky but not nearly as dangerous as giving up on love and belonging and joy - the experiences that make us the most vulnerable. Only when we are brave enough to explore the darkness will we discover the infinite power of our light." (3.)

Mindful Prompt: The safest place you can be can also feel like the riskiest. But it's not risk you're feeling, it's vulnerability. Even though it feels raw and scary, if you sink beneath the surface of things, you'll also feel the hum and pulse of possibility. Only when you are brave enough to go all-in with your life will you discover you are strong to live it.

SAFETY FIRST - PART 3
Breaking Open Is How You Heal

Heartbreak will not kill you like you think it will; like it feels like it will. When you're in its grip and it's throwing you around, it seems sure that you will not survive the next turn.

But you will.

I'm not saying you should seek it, or anything sadistic like that. The fact is, you won't have to. Heartbreak will find you on its own easily enough.

I am saying: you do not have to fear it.

We fear being broken like we fear physical pain because it disrupts our comfort and our ideas of success and blessing and what a good life looks like. You've been conditioned to believe that security and safety come in things like accomplishment, ease, and triumph.

But safety doesn't live in those transient, here-today-gone-tomorrow, places.

Hardening your heart is completely unsafe, even if it doesn't feel like it. The urge to wall up, and become rigid, can often be confused as strength because it looms large and heavy. Hardening your heart may keep you from feeling some pain, it may keep you upright a little longer, it may give the illusion of strength and that you're holding it together. But a hard heart shatters into a thousand pieces, making the fall out from heartbreak more complicated and difficult.

A soft heart? That feels every knock; that bruises and breaks open in places; that suffers from the sharp, cruel corners of the world; that takes in sudden breaths and holds them without knowing; that laughs till it hurts and is struck down by beauty and feels like love just might blow it to pieces?

A soft heart feels and bends and opens... it doesn't shatter. That's why the prophet wrote so poetically that God said:

"I will give you a new heart, and a new spirit I will put within you. And I will remove the heart of stone from your flesh and give you a heart of flesh." (4.)

Let the weight of heartbreak settle within you when it comes. Your heart was made to break, said Oscar Wilde. Which isn't a sad thing at all. Your heart in its natural state, is capable of carrying the weight of its own brokenness all the way to your healing. It's a muscle, after all, and to grow and strengthen, muscles need to tear and repair, tear and repair, tear and repair.

This is where you are most safe. Not in the absence of heartbreak, but in your capacity and willingness to live your way through it.

Mindful Prompt: Mary Oliver wrote, *"I tell you this to break your heart, to which I mean only that it break open and never close again to the rest of the world."* (5.) Breaking open is how you heal.

SAFETY FIRST - PART 4

In Over Your Head

There is a way, despite all the odds, to keep your heart safe. It's not a place. You cannot buy or acquire or earn it.

It's a state of living that you enter into.

Some say that God keeps them safe. There are a heap of scriptures that seem to say the same thing, too.

Like this one:
"The angel of the Lord encamps around those who fear God, and God delivers them. Taste and see that the Lord is good; blessed is the one who takes refuge in God." (6.)

(Hedge of protection anybody? #triggered.)

And this one:
"The name of the Lord is a fortified tower; the righteous run to it and are safe." (7.)

Annnnd this one:
"The Lord will keep you from all harm, God will watch over your life; the Lord will watch over your coming and going both now and forevermore." (8.)

Apparently, all you need to do to be safe is be a Christian. There you go, done. Safe. Protected. Free from harm. Hedged in. Watched over.

Has that been your experience? Has God kept you safe from heartbreak? Has God kept you safe from financial pressure or trouble? Relationship uncertainty and change and pain? Have the bullies been silenced? Have the illnesses and afflictions and diseases disappeared? Are you immune to viruses and bacteria? Are your loved ones unaffected by suffering? Are you?

Here's another verse for you:
"When you're in over your head, I'll be there with you. When you're in rough waters, you will not go down. When you're between a rock and a hard place, it won't be a dead end. Because I am God, your personal God, the Holy of Israel, your Savior." (9.)

This is not a verse about God being like Jiminy Cricket, or the Fairy Godmother, or an entity that stays with some and not with others according to their behaviour.

This is about alignment. The Divine Path is one of survival and thriving; it's where you go through the water and the flames and the rocky places, and you come out the other side because you trust and believe that you can. The spiritual path is one of resilience. Nearly every time you read a scripture about God giving someone strength, or being a place of safety and refuge, or being an entity of protection and power, the author was in the thick of life themselves. They were in over their head, surrounded by flames, climbing over mountains of impossibility.

Which, I might add, is the only way to get through to the other side; you've got to keep going. There is a degree of safety in never leaving home. But it keeps you small, isolated, and separate from the expansive and divine life you were created for. It's not really safe at all, because it keeps you from becoming all that the waters and fires and mountains make you.

When you align your spirit and heart with the Divine Path, with the way of resilience, with trust and grace and grit and faith, you will live on. You will make it through. Yes, perhaps in ways you never thought, and things may look very different than you imagined on the other side. But if you open your heart, and submit to the grace available to you at every moment, you will rise. You'll look back at what you thought was extremely precarious and unsafe and risky to see that it made you stronger, wiser, and more beautiful and that you were capable of doing hard things, after all.

That is the safest place you can be.

Mindful Prompt: There is no such thing as a ruined life. The raw materials for wonder and healing are always at your fingertips, waiting for direction, waiting for you to rise and get to work. As Shane Koyczan said: *"If your heart is broken, make art with the pieces."*

SAFETY FIRST - PART 5

Your Body Is A Safe Place

The safest place for you to be is at home in your body.

When you practice self-acceptance, love, and belonging, a whole realm of peace and safety opens up within you that transcends anything else that is happening to you and outside of you.

Maybe you were raised to believe that your heart is wicked, untrustworthy, wretched and nothing without Jesus. Maybe you were taught that the only safety you would ever be able to find was outside of yourself, in heaven far, far, away, and only those who call upon the name of the Lord in the way that the powers that be tell you to, will have protection and a place of refuge. As a result of these toxic theologies, that painfully tear you asunder, causing you to divorce yourself from your body, maybe you don't feel safe within your own skin.

But friend, your body is for you, not against you. Mental illness is not a weakness; the physical differences you have compared to your peers is not, or shouldn't be, something that sets you lower than others; your illness and things you struggle with in your body is a mystery not an indictment; your face and features, no matter what you think of them or how others describe them, are wonderful and beautiful and holy. You are your body and your body is you and you are a holy and divine being created by love, for love, with the capacity to love and wonder and become and live an expansive, full life.

It's true.

The safest place you can be is at home in your body.

Embrace your skin and bones and flesh and blood like a holy temple, a house - they are a part of you as much as your thoughts and words and ideas and goals are.

Belonging to yourself is the safest place you can be.

When you belong to yourself, you won't try to extract your validity and self-worth and sense of space from other people, or experiences, or a certain set of circumstances. Belonging to yourself is how you become free. Belonging to yourself is how you become empowered to take responsibility for your life and show up to it. Belonging to yourself is how you heal and transcend pain into wonder and joy.

Jeremiah (1) and the Psalmist (139) wrote that you were known and seen and heard and loved long before you were born. You were not birthed into this world to become someone that you are not. The journey of your life is to become fully yourself, and to find your home within.

God does not save you from yourself; the Divine saves you to yourself, from having to be anyone but your truest and deepest self; from the hell of living torn in two, trying to attain your holiness rather than just owning it. All the suffering in the world is born of people and ideas who are trying to find a place to belong while having a scarcity mindset about themselves and the abundance of the world. But you belong to yourself, to God who is within you at home already. That's what being redeemed and restored and renewed means: a return to who you really are; coming home, and finding that you were always there.

You are safe, here, in your body. There may be pain, there may be trauma, there may be uncertainty and distrust and even disdain held within your cells. But the way to heal them is not by abandoning them, shouting declarations at them, blaming and shaming and disguising and belittling, no. The way to wholeness is love and compassion and grace and truth, for you, to you, and about you, from yourself.

You are safe here, if you want to be, if you choose it, if you take that step of faith and believe it.

Mindful Prompt: Take a moment, find what feels good (thank you, Adrienne), and close your eyes. Unclench your jaw. Relax your forehead. Let your shoulders and arms and hips release. Breathe in long and slow. Imagine that you're taking in for yourself love, grace, compassion, and goodness. You are bestowing upon yourself a physical and spiritual blessing. Receive it. Breathe out long and true. Let it all go. Breathe out all those hateful and limiting beliefs you have about yourself. Repeat as needed.

BELONGING TO YOURSELF IS HOW YOU BECOME
EMPOWERED TO TAKE RESPONSIBILITY FOR YOUR LIFE
AND SHOW UP TO IT. BELONGING TO YOURSELF IS HOW
YOU HEAL AND TRANSCEND PAIN INTO WONDER AND JOY.

SAFETY FIRST - PART 6

A Safe Invitation

Safety is a shared experience.

The way to safety amongst us is first to create a safe place within yourself. A group of people that doesn't need to take safety from each other to find safety for themselves; that understands that there is more than enough to go around; that is secure in themselves and does not need validation from another or to have dominion over another to take up their own space, is a safe community.

Frederick Buechner said:
"Compassion is the sometimes fatal capacity for feeling what it's like to live inside somebody else's skin. It is the knowledge that there can never really be any peace and joy for me until there is peace and joy finally for you too." (11.)

Safety at the expense of someone else isn't safety at all.

Here-in lies the great tension in this messy world we live in, where it's easy to feel like we're in the biggest global standoff you could imagine. It's like we are all collectively waiting to see who will fire first; we're armed, we're ready, and we're damn sure that we have the right to be. Safe in the most unsafe way.

Imagine a world where there is no standoff? Where we are quick to forgive and reach out and help. Where borders act more as healthy boundaries and places of connection, then prison lines of entitlement and bias, keeping some in, and others out. Imagine a world where we were truly safe to love and be loved.

Safety is a shared experience. And we will only get there, not by weapons or wealth, but by grace and compassion.

The Psalmist wrote,

"Some trust in chariots and some in horses, but we trust in the name of the Lord our God." (12.)

When this Psalm was written, the nation of Israel was at a turning point. They were literally buying chariots and horses (in this day and age that would translate to weapons and armoury) to boost their military power and capacity. The author here is challenging its readers, asking them what kind of life did they want? What kind of safety were they going to go after? What kind of presence did they want to be in the world?

The name of God was a way of talking about the essence of divinity in Ancient Hebrew culture. Nothing magical happens when you mention God as a name or a title or a label. It's a way of speaking about what you're going to align with. The essence of divinity is love and grace and compassion, where strength and safety are shared experiences beginning in the heart and growing outward toward each other. It's holistic and organic, not performative or reactionary.

The name of God carries the truth that there is no peace for one, unless there is peace for everyone.

It's not an indictment on us. It's not a condemnation on who we are and who we have been. It's an invitation, a welcoming, a reminder, to wake up and discover and connect to ourselves, and each other.

How else do we find God but in finding and loving ourselves and one another?

Mindful Prompt: Instead of seeing peace as something that you earn, or win, or acquire, or take, remind yourself that peace is already accessible to you. It's within you, around you, a part of you. It's something that you cultivate and become and live into. It begins with you and spills out into the world around you.

SAFETY FIRST - PART 7

The Safest Place You Can Be Is Right Here

Safety happens where you don't think it does.

When you think of what it means to be safe, do you imagine places of physical security? Where you are hemmed in and protected and comfortable? Do you picture being with people who will never lie or cheat or hurt or fail?

Sometimes, in the name safety, you live small and restricted. But that is no safe place for your heart or life, and the bigness and expansiveness you were created for. Sometimes the safest place you can be is out on a limb, taking a step of faith, risking it all to be who you are and show up for those you love.

Most of the time, when people say they want safety, what they're really talking about is control.

Safety is not found in controlling things and people and events and seasons and outcomes. Control of any kind is an illusion. It keeps you small, and ultimately, incredibly unsafe. It's a narrative that we really want to be true, but time and time again fails us. It doesn't matter how many walls you build, how carefully you curate an experience, how much insurance you have physically and/or metaphorically, life always gets through the cracks and upsets controls equilibrium.

It's a waste of time protecting yourself from heartbreak. It will find its way to you no matter how well you try to avoid it. It's the nature of things. However, you can let the weight of heartbreak settle within you when it comes. Your heart was made to break. This is not a bad thing or something to grieve. Your heart in its natural state is capable of carrying the weight of its own brokenness all the way to your healing. It's a muscle, after all, and to grow and strengthen, muscles need to tear and repair, tear and repair, tear and repair.

There is wisdom in creating and finding a safe place for you to live, to be safe with your choices and your body and your love and your loves. But wisdom herself will tell you that you can never be sure, that's why you can only walk the spiritual path of resilience and trust by faith and grace. And you can trust faith and grace to see you through.

Because that is where you are most safe. When you belong to yourself so fiercely you don't need to take from anyone else to sure up your end of the bargain; when you wake up to our communal belonging to each other, the oneness that permeates you and me and things and the earth; when we give and we share and become along side each other with each other, rather than at the expense or the pain of the other, you will be living yourself into freedom in real time.

You are safe within resilience, self-acceptance, mercy, compassion, and union. Which doesn't mean that you are safe from hardship. That kind of safety only fosters ignorance and naivety, which creates dangerous places for you and those around you.

The world is big and scary and wonderful and unpredictable. The Divine is stitched into the fabric of everything and everyone everywhere. There is nowhere that you can go, no experience you can have, no set of circumstances you can find yourself in, where you will

be separate from the safety of Divine Love that leads you on, and shows you that you have the capacity to do hard things, and to even find joy and bliss and peace while doing them.

You have to flip it - your understanding of safety - to something that sounds more like what Rumi said: *"Run from what's comfortable. Forget safety. Live where you fear to live. Destroy your reputation. Be notorious."*

Safety first, now and always. The safest place you can be is at home in your body; the safest place you can be is when you have nothing to prove, and nothing to earn. The safest place you can be is where you accept the love and grace sitting unwrapped at your feet waiting for you, without asking whether or not you deserve it.

The safest place you can be is wide awake, heart open, here and now.

Mindful Prompt: "Your deepest fear is not that you are inadequate, but that you are powerful beyond measure. It is your light, not your darkness that most frightens you. You ask yourself, 'Who am I to be brilliant, gorgeous, talented, fabulous?' Actually, who are you not to be? You are a child of God. Your playing small does not serve the world. You were born to make manifest the glory of God that is within you. As you are liberated from your own fear, your presence automatically liberates others." Marianne Williamson (13).

"LOVE IS NOT SOMETHING YOU DO; LOVE IS SOMEONE YOU ARE. IT IS YOUR TRUE SELF. LOVE IS WHERE YOU CAME FROM AND LOVE IS WHERE YOU'RE GOING."

Richard Rohr

STAND IN YOUR POWER - PART 1

Who's Power Is It?

"With great power there must also come great responsibility," wrote Stan Lee. This series was inspired by my son, Sam, who has quoted these words to me from the time he started reading Spider-Man when he was a small boy.

Perhaps we are so quick to misappropriate our power, shrug it off, step away from it, deny it, demonise it,

become disempowered, because of the responsibility it seems to need. To stand in your power, and own your own life, means that you must take responsibility for it, in the good and the bad.

It's actually what God wants for you. Divine intention - God's will for your life, as some would say - is that you show up to it, own it, and live it.

You were not created to be in a co-dependent spiritual relationship with a man in the sky who answers prayers according to your ability to behave in line with a certain standard that has been interpreted and pedalled around, predominately by old white men for the last few centuries. That is just as toxic as co-dependent relationships with other people.

You were created to stand on your own two feet. You were created to use your autonomy as a means for connection. You were designed with a brain capable of making decisions, a body capable of feeling and living and moving and breathing, in all the varying abilities and ways our bodies feel and live and move and breathe. You were made with the inherent power to live your own life.

Yes, yes you were.

Religion and spirituality that teaches otherwise, wants to control you for its own gain.

The Psalmist said:
"[God] lifted me out of the miry pit, the slimy clay, and set my feet on a rock, steadied my legs." (1.)

Maybe you grew up believing that your feet would always shake and waver unless you believed a certain thing, lived a certain way, and stood in certain places defined by people who don't know you, or your situation, or what this verse was trying to convey when it was written and recorded by our Ancient Jewish Mothers and Fathers.

Whatever miry and slimy place you feel you are slipping and falling into and through, you will find your feet again. God lifts you out of these places, but not through some divine miracle that takes you instantly from fallen to standing. God lifts you through the power of your own life, showing you that you can do it, revealing that you were created to do it, and believing that you can and will do it, every step of the way.

Most studies on this verse in Psalm 40 focus on what the miry clay is (what sins and evils and fires and tribulations you get tangled up in) and what the rock is (Jesus and good deeds and Christian living and being right and all those fundamental things). But I want to focus on the going-from-being-on-your-butt-to-standing part.

But it's God who does it, I hear some of you say. It's God who picks you up; lifts you out of the poop-hole that you got yourself into. It is God who makes the difference. It is God who is strong. It is God who makes me stand.

To which I say yes. But it's also you.

It's not binary. It's not one or the other. It's yes and yes. God uses your own life to save you. God lifts you out of the miry clay the same way that blood pumps through your body, messages fire in your brain through to your nervous system to your thighs and legs and feet, and you find yourself standing... God uses you - your flesh and blood life - to do God's work. It's a partnership, a participatory relationship. It's God's power, and your power, which are together, not separate. A creative, life generating force, that works together for the health and empowerment of you, and the world around you.

Mindful Prompt: What will you do with this power that you have? With your responsibility? How does it make you feel? Remember, it's power with, not power over, or instead of. God is for you. You may as well be, too.

STAND IN YOUR POWER - PART 2

There Is No Top

I'm not entirely sure that power corrupts in and of itself. There are plenty of people with power who are not corrupt and use their power for good. And if ultimate power ultimately corrupts, then what about The Divine? And how can you tell? What measuring stick can we use to assess those in power whether they work for good or evil?

It's never just one thing. Good and bad is grey. We are complicated beings, full of all kinds of things; damage and trauma, but also grace and light. Who gets to say where and what the line is?

There are other things at play, too, like fear, greed, hatred, anger... Rather than being a world that suffers from thinking too much of itself, there's an epidemic of people and institutions and governments who don't know how to stand in their own power - in their collective True Self - who don't know how to love themselves, who don't know how to care for their own hearts. Instead, they live from their ego, their False Self, desperately trying to fill the void.

We are (by and large) too busy trying to war and money and polarise and earn and convince and manipulate and trick and work our way to the top, to realise that we were always meant to stand on our own two feet, together. Side by side. There is no top.

Standing in your power doesn't corrupt you. It doesn't make you a sinner. It doesn't make you selfish or egotistical. It doesn't inflate your sense of self or make you flakey or set you apart from God as though you don't need God to stand.

Standing in your own power is not about being in a position of power over other people and things and situations. It's simply about taking responsibility for your own life - do what you can with what you have; being you're truest self with your whole self. It's about standing on your own two feet. No hiding or pacifying, no pretending or excusing or ignoring.

All you, all here, right now.

John Philip Newell said:

"Christ comes to reawaken us to our true nature. He is our epiphany. He comes to show us the face of God. He comes to also show us our face, the true face of the human soul... Grace is given to reconnect us to our true nature. Grace is opposed not to what is deepest in us but to what is false in us. It is given to restore us to the core of our being and to free us from the unnaturalness of what we are doing to each other and to the earth." (2.)

The Psalmist wrote:
"[God] lifted me out of the miry pit, the slimy clay, and set my feet on a rock, steadied my legs." (3.)

God lifted YOU, set you on YOUR feet, and steadied YOUR legs, so YOU could stand.

Stand as you are, who you are, in all that you are.

This kind of power is generative and connective. It's healing and wholesome. It has courage and grit and compassion.

Seneca said:
"Most powerful is he who has himself in his own power."

You don't have to choose between God's power and your power. It makes religious people uncomfortable when you start talking about standing in your truth, or in your power, because they think it opposes God's. But there is only power. Not God's or yours or theirs. There is only power and what you choose to do with it. It's not a fight between you and the Divine... it's something God wants to share with you... after all, you've been set on your feet so you can walk your own path.

With God. With others. Together.

Mindful Prompt: Take a moment, close your eyes, follow your breath. Sink into it. Find the centre of yourself, the place where you feel most grounded and connected to the infinite. Imagine a spark of energy, the life force, bloom in that place. That sense of power? It's you and God together, integrated, connected, working and being together - like your breath - like you were always meant to.

"OWNING YOUR OWN STORY IS THE BRAVEST THING
YOU WILL EVER DO." - BRENÉ BROWN.

STAND IN YOUR POWER - PART 3

It Is Yours

Brené Brown said:
"Owning your own story is the bravest thing you will ever do."

That's what it means to stand on your own two feet. As Anne Lamott wrote:
"You own everything that has happened to you." (3.)

It is yours. It is yours. It is yours.

Your life is yours.

No, it's not God's. As in, it's not not God's if you claim it as your own. It's not one or the other. Your life is your own just as much as it is God's, in the same way that your body is your own but unless it is filled with breath, it remains lifeless.

There's a misunderstanding in some spiritual communities and spaces and traditions that mandates that in order to have a 'relationship with Divinity' you have to give up control and autonomy of your own life. You hear people talk about how they waited and asked God what to do. Which is fine. You hear people say that they read their Bibles and interpreted what to do from the text. Which is fine. You hear people say that they went to their Pastor or leader and asked them what they should do. Which is fine.

But at the end of the day, after you've prayed and waited and read and asked and put out your fleeces and sought the prophets and made a sacrifice on your altar...

You are still the one engaging your body and senses and brain and heart in whatever it is YOU decide to do next.

It is YOUR life. It will be more impactful and meaningful and true if you decide to own it for yourself.

Stand in your power. The place that Christ wants you to be - not in the mire of confusion and indecision and the inability to take responsibility for your own self. Your life. Your power. Standing. On solid rock. Yep. That's where Christ leads you, that's where you were made to stand. And that is where you stand with Divinity coursing through you. It is not your strength or God's strength; it's all the strength happening at the same time within you.

Mindful Prompt: What happens if you feel like you are in the mire, in the pit, with no foreseeable way out? It turns out there is always a way, and the Divine works with you and in you so that you are the one who ends up finding your own brave way out. You are the one you've been waiting for all this time.

STAND IN YOUR POWER - PART 4
The Universe Is Entirely Relational

You were created to stand in your power.

But what happens if you feel like you're on your butt and you can't, for the life of you, seem to find a way to get back up again?

Firstly, let me say this: you can rest on your own two feet, you don't have to always be moving. It's metaphorical, ya'll. Taking responsibility for your own self-care is a huge component of this.

If you find, at any time and during anything, that it's hard to stand on your own, ask for help. That's why we are here together in the world. We are integrated connective beings for a reason.

There is no shame in it. When you ask for help and receive it, or when someone asks you for help, and you give it, you are participating in the natural way of things. We stand on our two feet, together. Side by side, helping each other, needing each other, wanting to be with each other.

That's how this whole thing works. When you think of God as a relationship of three, in the language of Father, Son, and Spirit (Parent, Child, Spirit), you can see that pattern of three work between us, too: you, me, Divinity. Harmony is created when we allow the relationship between the three to flow.

Richard Rohr said:
"The energy in the universe is not in the planets, or in the protons or neutrons, but in the relationship between them. Not in the particles but in the space between them. Not in the cells of organisms but in the way the cells feed and give feedback to one another. Not in any precise definition of the three persons of the Trinity as much as in the relationship between the Three! This is where all the power for infinite renewal is at work: The loving relationship between them. The infinite love between them. The dance itself. In other words, it is an entirely relational universe." (5.)

There will be times when you need help. And there will be times when someone will need your help. Help keeps us connected. It keeps us together. It keeps us working and moving and living and breathing side by side. Help is the way this all works.

So, ask for it.

If you're on your ass and you can't get up, that's ok. Sometimes life is really hard. You were never meant to be able to get up on your own all the time. In fact, I think in order to get on your feet, steady your legs, and stand in your power, more often than not you're going to have to reach your hand out to a steadying and supportive entity. Isn't that grace? That we're here for one another? For each other?

And yeah, maybe you'll receive a whiz-bang instantaneous miracle from God-self that beams down from heaven like it would out of Harry Potter's wand and changes things in a flash of lightning and rainbows and all of a sudden you'll be on your feet wearing Yeezys and singing hallelujah.

Or maybe the miracle you need will come through someone else. Through asking and receiving, seeking and finding, knocking on a closed door and having it open up to you. We were created to be the vehicle of miracles to each other. So let the miracles flow.

Mindful Prompt: It takes asking and receiving and giving - the relationship between the three. They are a grace so sweet and full and true, you'll be back on your feet before you know it.

STAND IN YOUR POWER - PART 5

Love Is Someone You Are

Your body and spirit were made in such a way that you need to stand in your power to access and engage the fullness of them.

I know sometimes you think that it would be easier to stand in your power if you looked like them, or had their experience, or access to those resources, or were educated to this level, or had more happiness in your childhood, or if that hadn't happened to you, and, well, if you were an entirely different person.

'I could stand in my power if (fill in the blank)...' is a place we've all been.

Here's the thing: believing that you can't stand with what you've got and what you've been given will have you on your butt in no time. And the only way to get back up from this kind of fall is self-love and acceptance.

Which is hard for a few reasons.

Self-love and acceptance are challenging because we've all done things we are ashamed of, things we knew were wrong, things that have hurt others, things that we would not accept from another person.

Self-love and acceptance are difficult because when life cracks us open, we don't like what we find. Whether it be hardness, bitterness, a personality trait, a reflex, a limiting belief we can't shake, or memories and experiences that have left us twisted and wounded... when confronted with ourselves, it's sometimes hard to love what we find.

Self-love and acceptance are hard because we've been taught systematically by some factions of religion, consumerism, pop culture, politics and policies, and more, that we simply are not worthy of self-love and acceptance. And even worse, that to love and accept ourselves would leave us unhinged and abandoned to our own evil inclinations and desires.

But dear one, is that working for you? A life disassociating your heart and body and mind from your own love and acceptance? Self-hatred and non-acceptance don't make you holy. It's a conduit of pain and makes you lonely and full of sorrow.

Mark Twain said:
"The worst loneliness is to not be comfortable with yourself."

Rupi Kaur said:
"How you love yourself is how you teach others to love you." (6.)

Brené Brown said:
"True belonging only happens when we present our authentic, imperfect selves to the world, our sense of belonging can never be greater than our level of self-acceptance." (7.)

EE Cummings said:
"Once we believe in ourselves, we can risk curiosity, wonder, spontaneous delight, or any experience that reveals the human spirit."

Richard Rohr said:
"Love is not something you do; love is someone you are. It is your True Self. Love is where you came from and love is where you're going. It's not something you can buy. It's not something you can attain. It is the presence of God within you, called the Holy Spirit—or what some theologians name uncreated grace. We can't diminish God's love for us. What we can do, however, is learn how to believe it, receive it, trust it, allow it, and celebrate it, accepting Trinity's whirling invitation to join in the cosmic dance...

[buckle in, because this could change your life]

The very nature of God is to seek out the deepest possible communion and friendship with every last creature on this earth. That's the job description of God. That's what it's all about. And the only thing that can keep you out of this divine dance is fear and doubt, or any self-hatred. What would happen in your life—right now—if you accepted what God has created and even allowed? Suddenly, this is a very safe universe. You have nothing to be afraid of. God is for you. God is leaping toward you! God is on your side, honestly more than you are on your own." (8.)

Mindful Prompt: You will not become overrun by evil if you let love well up inside of you for your own life. It's already in you, willing you to stand, wanting to heal you. You just have to accept it, and allow it.

STAND IN YOUR POWER - PART 6

Figure It Out As You Go

Life has a way of making you feel powerless, knocking you off your feet, down, to the floor, on the ground, in all kinds of mess. Sometimes you need to reach out for help to get back up again. Sometimes you need to learn to be where you are and love yourself upright again.

And sometimes, you just need to get back up.

Coco Channel (I know, I was just as surprised as you are) said:
"How many cares one loses when one decides not to be something but to be someone."

Decide not to do something, but to be someone. Maybe you struggle to stand in your power because you think it's about doing and not about being. Always, and forever, be yourself. Live your story. Walk your path. It's confusing, I know. Because all around you are

people standing and walking and doing and it can seem like you need to do what they're doing to get where they're going.

But all you have to do to stand in your power is be yourself.

Alice Walker said:
"The most common way people give up their power is by thinking they don't have any."

You have power. You have power in your lungs and blood and bones and breath and body and heart and mind. You have agency and (most of you) have choice. You have your voice and your story and your own time.

This is your gig. No one else's. Not your partner's or your sister's or your father's or your friend's.

Yours.

Paul wrote to his friend, Timothy, and said:
"God did not give us a spirit of fear, but rather a spirit of power and of love and of self-discipline." (9.)

You have the power, the love, and the self-discipline (which is the result of self-acceptance and love), to stand in your power, and do the work.

I get it. Sometimes, when you're flat on your back, it can feel like you have anything but the power and the will to get back to your feet again, to a place of power and agency. And if you're in this state long enough for whatever reason, the longing to get upright can begin to wane. But you were made for standing and walking and moving and being alive in this world. And sometimes the only thing that will get you back up again is to do it. Take the leap. Even though it's hard, even though it hurts. Even though it may seem undignified and embarrassing and like you don't know what you're doing, get back up, and stand in your own glorious power.

Ralph Waldo Emerson.
"Do the thing and you will have the power."

The power comes as you go, not as you wait. A leap of faith isn't a leap if you know you can make the jump before you take off. It's scary, contemplating doing something you're not sure you know how to do, or that you can even do. But God is with you and in you not to create an atmosphere of fear, but to fan into flame the power, love and self-discipline you have within you to do what you need to do.

If it takes forgiveness, forgive - yourself, or others, or God, or life... step by step, bit by bit, figure it out as you go.

If it takes courage, be strong. Little by slowly, step by step, courage begets courage, and is only courage when you engage it scared out of your skin. Figure it out as you go.

If it takes faith, then it takes faith, and you will have to accept the fact that you don't know, and you can't be sure, and you just need to move your feet and your legs and your bottom and your chest and your arms in such as way as to bring you upright (metaphorical FYI).

Everyone, forever and always, no matter what resources they have or don't have, have figured it out step by step, on the way, as they go.

Mindful Prompt: You can do this, and you will do this, and as you go about doing the work of standing, you will find that you have the power to stand, on your own two feet. And you'll call it a miracle.

STAND IN YOUR POWER - PART 7

Get Up And Live

The prophet Habakkuk wrote:
"The Lord God is my strength. God has made my feet steady and sure like hinds' feet and makes me walk forward with spiritual confidence on my high places of challenge and responsibility." (10.)

A hind is an animal that can walk seemingly impossible trails (that don't even look like trails) on mountains and cliffs so high up it would make your head spin, and your lungs ache. Habakkuk was using this as a picture for his own life. God enabled/empowered/created him to walk, with confidence, in places of challenge and responsibility and hardship on his own two feet.

Life is wonderful and tricky, hard and glorious, blissful and painful, and we were made to traverse all its wild and unpredictable landscapes on our own two feet, side by side, together. Things may happen to you that are not your fault, that land you on your ass. Or you might get yourself into a whole lot of trouble on your own accord. Either way, your happiness, engagement, impact, and healing are your own personal responsibility.

You have the power to own it, to own your own life. To forgive and love and question and rage and laugh and work and gaze at the wonder of it all.

God loves you. The Divine is for you. The ground of

being is beneath you. The source of all life is in you. Even still, the level to which you truly experience all that life has for you to live... is up to you.

Your kids can't do it for you.
Your parents can't do it for you.
Your partner can't do it for you.
Your best friends can't do it for you.
Your boss, barista, pastor, guru, chiropractor, or therapist can't do it for you.
Not even God can live your life for you.

The power is yours. And so is the love. And so are the two feet at the end of your legs upon which you stand.

And just like the hind in Habakkuk 3, you can, and you will make it. You will walk those impossible trails up the side of impossible mountains and arrive at impossible destinations with the most impossible views.

You will do that.
You have the power to get yourself there.
All you have to do is get up and start living.

Mindful Prompt: Stand in your power. Be who you are, troubles, challenges, strengths, failures, wounds, and all. It all belongs. It's all glorious. It's all yours.

"LIKE THE JOY OF THE SEA
COMING HOME TO SHORE,
MAY THE RELIEF OF
LAUGHTER RINSE THROUGH
YOUR SOUL."

John O'Donohue.

JOY IS A WILD, WILD THING - PART 1

Joy Will Save You In The End

Who owns the market on joy?

To varying degrees, joy has been turned into a commodity. A thing. Something that you can attain and hoard and lock away. Something you buy or manufacture. Something you can control.

But wild things can't be controlled.

Joy are the vines taking human-made structures back down into the earth. Joy are the waves crashing on the shore wearing away rock and bringing new treasures with it each and every time. Joy are the birds that nest in your ceiling and the ants that crawl through your kitchen no matter what you do to stop them. Joy is an eight-year-old girl dancing in the mirror while dreaming impossible dreams that might one day come true. Joy are the tears that fall from an old man's face as he grips the photo of the one he loves who is no longer there with him. Joy is the womb opening, readying for birth - it cannot be stopped, it cannot be slowed, it follows its own natural chaos as it brings forth life.

Joy is a wild, wild thing.

How do you find it?

Can joy exist in global pandemics while lives are fought for and lost and changed forever? When careers are toppled, and jobs dry up? Can joy exist when BIPOC still can't go for a run or a walk without being killed for no other reason than the ridiculous and untrue narratives that raise eyebrows and guns alike? Can joy exist while they and them are denied their human right to be who they are and live in the world as they are? Can joy exist while children are dying and mothers are hurting, and fathers are struggling... can joy exist when the (some) church(es) continually says "all are welcome," and then persist to uphold, perpetuate and practice exclusivity?

The book of Nehemiah is a record of the rebuilding of Jerusalem and the return of exiles from Babylon under the leadership of Ezra and Nehemiah. When the walls and towns had finally been restored, and the people settled into their new homes and lives, they celebrated with rituals and feasts. Nehemiah said:

"This day is holy to our Lord. Do not grieve, for the joy of the Lord is your strength." (1.)

We've been conditioned to think that joy is the reward - it comes at the end if you've worked hard enough and if you've been good enough. But joy is your fuel - the precious and wild joy of being alive, here and now.

We suffer, and we grieve because on some holy and fundamental level, we want to be here, we like being here, and we love the people we're here with. We get frustrated and angry because we care and are attached and have desire and longing because, at the foundation of it all, the simple joy of being here in the world is wrapped around our heart and body like a vine that grows of its own accord.

Khalil Gibran said:
"The deeper that sorrow carves into your being, the more joy you can contain. Is not the cup that holds your wine the very cup that was burned in the potter's oven? And is not the lute that soothes your spirit, the very wood that was hollowed with knives? When you are joyous, look deep into your heart and you shall find it is only that which has given you sorrow that is giving you joy. When you are sorrowful look again in your heart, and you shall see that in truth you are weeping for that which has been your delight." (2.)

Oscar Wilde said:
"A flower blossoms for its own joy."

There's a natural cadence to joy. It exists not because of what happens, but inside of everything that happens. It is part of the fabric of the universe. Too long have we tried to tame joy, while at the same time, we have gloried in our sufferings, without letting them both take up their own wild and true space.

Joy is going to save you. Commit to finding it again and letting it grow wild, as it should be, as it is.

Mindful Prompt: Journey within, and see if you find that place where grief and joy meet. Think of something that fills you with sorrow. Dig into that feeling - why is the sorrow there? Keep looking until you find the joy - the thing or person or experience that made you glad.

JOY IS A WILD, WILD THING - PART 2
Joy Is A Shared Experience

It is not selfish to want to be happy and find your bliss. What's the alternative? Cultivating a life of pain and sorrow? Those things will find you no matter what you do. Seeking happiness is not wrong, as long as it's not at someone else's expense.

Happiness tends to be triggered by external factors and influences - winning, achieving, attaining, being affirmed, receiving... But joy? JD Salinger said:

"Happiness is a solid, joy is a liquid." (3.)

Happiness can too easily become stagnant, while joy has a wild and holy flow to it.

In Ancient Hebrew, the word for joy is simcha. In the Torah, simcha was not an individual experience; it had a collective quality. It's not something to be won, but something to be shared.

In his book, Nehemiah, and his friend Ezra, were reading the words of the revelation (not the one that we know from the Biblical text...) out to their people. They had finished rebuilding Jerusalem, and many exiles had returned to the beloved city. But as the words washed over them, the people grieved - the weight of the words filled them with sorrow. Nehemiah said to them:

"Go home and prepare a feast, holiday food and drink; and share it with those who don't have anything: This day is holy to God. Don't feel bad. The joy of God is your strength!" (4.)

The joy was in their shared experience: in the drinking and eating and celebrating; sharing with those who had nothing, everyone at the table, no-one missing out. This kind of joy? This kind of celebrating? This kind of

sharing and including and togetherness?

There's a wild and uncontainable strength in that.

Frederick Buechner said:
"Wherever people love each other and are true to each other and take risks for each other, God is with them and for them and they are doing God's will." (5.)

The ancient Jewish people knew how to celebrate no matter what they were going through. Alan King once said that every Jewish holiday could be summed up as: "They tried to kill us. We survived! Let's eat!" The rituals and traditions they observed, and still do, gave strength to their joy; gave it structure and form and practice. The power of joy comes from its communal nature. It's not focused on the individual attaining or achieving something outside of itself. But on collective sharing and cooperating; giving of oneself to others in a circular manner.

Joy blooms out of what you believe about yourself, others, and the world. It comes when you make peace with who are you, how you are, why you are, and what you have to give rather than what you can take.

Happiness is a solid. You can pursue it, hold onto it, hoard it, pop it on the mantlepiece. And you can acquire many different items of happiness over the course of a life. But joy is liquid; all you can do is let it flow and pour it from glass to glass.

Mindful Prompt: When you're with others, see if you can train yourself to notice the joy that buzzes in the foundation of things when people come together. Notice that as the Divine is in you, the Divine is in everyone you cross paths with. Accept it and allow it.

"MAKE PEACE WITH THE UNIVERSE.
TAKE JOY IN IT. IT WILL TURN TO
GOLD. RESSURECTION WILL BE NOW.
EVERY MOMENT, A NEW BEAUTY."

Rumi

JOY IS A WILD, WILD THING - PART 3

Every Moment, A New Beauty

Joy has no boundaries. It's a liquid. It leaks in even when all the doors and windows are tightly shut. It finds the holes in the ceiling, the cracks in the walls, and it comes in anyway. It's offensive like that. How can you feel anything like joy when someone you love is going through something unimaginable, or you are yourself? How can you laugh? How can you enjoy anything? Isn't that a betrayal of the pain? Of the sorrow?

Teilhard De Chardin said:
"Joy is the infallible sign of the presence of God."

The Psalmist wrote:
"You make known to me the path of life; in your presence, there is fullness of joy; at your right hand are pleasures forevermore." (6.)

In the Passion Translation, it reads: *"For you bring me a continual revelation of resurrection life, the path to the bliss that brings me face-to-face with you."* (7.)

Joy is that deep knowing that something truer, beyond your circumstances, is underneath it all and holds it all together. It's that greater presence in and through it all. *"Bliss brings me face to face with [God]."* Being present with God, the Divine energy that permeates the universe, is the essence of joy.

And that doesn't mean that you'll laugh hysterically, that your tears will dry up; that you'll behave in a manner contradictory to what you're going through. No. Joy sits in it with you, and keeps you present and awake to the all that is around you and in you. You can feel joy and sorrow at the same time without dishonouring anyone or anything.

This is hard to believe because we generally laugh at things and people, and not with them. We don't allow joy to bubble forth from our bodies, making sounds from our lips and movement in our limbs. Laughter has become a label, rather than allowed to be what it is: a release, an expression, a manifestation of something we have no words for.

Perhaps we need to re-wild our laughter. Joy is what will get us through pain, it's not what waits on the other side of it.

Rumi said:
"Make peace with the universe. Take joy in it. It will turn to gold. Resurrection will be now. Every moment, a new beauty."

There's no greater time for this bliss, this ultimate presence, then when pain seems to have taken up residence in your life. Here and now, at this moment, this tragic, horrific season that you're in, joy wants to flow, it wants to grow wild, it wants to set you free, not so that you become numb to your experience, but so you can live it, fully.

Frederick Buechner said:
"Joy is a mystery because it can happen anywhere, anytime, even under the most unpromising circumstances, even in the midst of suffering, with tears in its eyes..." (8.)

It's with tears in your eyes that joy does its most wild and miraculous work.

Mindful Prompt: Let it be. You don't need a reason for it. It doesn't need to be appropriate or proper or allowed. Let joy be. Don't be its master. Let it have its way. Let it grow the way it wants. Let it be wild and free. *"Like the joy of the sea coming home to shore, may the relief of laughter rinse through your soul."* John O'Donohue (9.)

JOY IS A WILD, WILD THING - PART 4

Bliss Can Be Your Teacher, Too

Often, the most tragic seasons of life teach you the most about who you are and why you are here. You'll hear "lean into the pain" almost daily in our house. Pain has long been my teacher.

Trauma and pain lead to growth, because in the moment of pain, in the grip of trauma, you have nowhere else to go. You either grow through it, or you stay small, shrunken in your grief.

Often, we wait until we suffer to make the changes we need in order to grow, because until we become uncomfortable, we're quite happy staying as is.

What if joy could be your teacher, too? What if you could grow because of, and through, the things that bring you bliss, just as much as the things that bring

you to your knees?

Glennon Doyle said:
"It seems easier for the world to love a suffering woman than it is for the world to love a joyful, confident woman." (10.)

Perhaps we distrust joy? Perhaps we glorify suffering? In our desperate need to not be alone in the pain we're in, we've made idols out of the pain of others. Think about it: what is your reaction when you see someone on the internet, on TV, at the shops, in your lounge room, standing confident and joyful and free?

Rarely do we want to high five those people. We want to knock them down a few pegs... we make up little scenarios and situations in our minds to comfort us in our comparison and jealousy: they must be hiding something, they must feel entitled, they must think they're better than the rest of us.

But maybe they just own their joy?

What if you let joy be the wild animal it is? What if you let it roar out from you? What if you let joy strengthen your back, and straighten your legs, and hold your head high? Why don't you let joy play a little? Have some fun?

What if you allowed joy to brings you to your knees in beauty and wonder and awe?

Perhaps we distrust joy because we think it's arrogant? Egotistical? Because we are afraid that if we let it be it will leave us and never come back? Because we are afraid it will lead us to sin, or to whimsy, or to wastefulness. But is anything that is done joyfully, a waste? And if joy is ultimate presence and connection with God and others, can it lead to sin? Is joy not holy? The Psalmist wrote that *"The nights of crying your eyes out give way to days of laughter."* (11.) They are both sacred. They both have the power to change you from the inside out.

What if you leaned into joy as well as pain; made it one of your teachers and guides; followed it all the way home, hugged it until your arms fell off; laughed with it until your voice wore away. What if you paid attention to joy like you do to pain?

What if we got around each other in joy, not just in pain, and championed one another? What if we gave ourselves to the wild ways of joy, just like we've learned to give ourselves to grief when it comes. Maybe, somewhere in the future, someone will discover the five stages of joy to help us wring as much healing and beauty and wonder out of it, too.

Maybe that's why the Biblical text talks so much about rejoicing... the practice of being joyful with our bodies.

Joy will heal you if you let it.

Mindful Prompt: Think back to a moment, experience, or person who has made you feel joyful. Stay with that memory. Let it rise in your body. Observe and engage those feelings. Let them wake you up. Let the healing flow.

JOY IS A WILD, WILD THING - PART 5

Practice Makes Progress

Joy can be practised. You can engage in rituals, exercises, all kinds of different things that will help you be able to find joy when you feel none and help you stay in joy when you find it.

In Nehemiah 8, the prophet told the people to *"Go home and prepare a feast, holiday food and drink; and share it with those who don't have anything: This day is holy to God. Don't feel bad. The joy of God is your strength!"*

Go home and throw a party. Practice joy. Make room for it. Set yourself up for it.

In what's considered the most depressing book of the Biblical text, the overarching theme of Ecclesiastes, ironically, is the practice of joy:

I know that there is nothing better for people than to rejoice and do good while they live (3:12).

So I saw that there is nothing better for a person than to rejoice in his work, because that is his lot (3:22).

So I commend rejoicing in life, because there is nothing better for a person under the sun than to eat and drink and rejoice (8:15).

However many years anyone may live, let him rejoice in them all (11:8).

When the author of Ecclesiastes wrote about the meaninglessness of life (Ecc 1), they didn't mean it in a pointless, empty, or futile way. The word used for meaningless is 'hevel,' and it means 'a shallow breath.' Ecclesiastes is a meditation on mortality - because life is so beautifully frail and quick, you should practice the most redemptive work you can:

Joy.

Gather and look and listen and touch and hold and laugh and eat and share and cry and be. Practice the joy of love. Practice the joy of looking after one another. Practice the joy of waking and the joy of sleeping. Practice joy in your body. Practice the wild and pure joy of being here in the world as you are.

It's a miracle, isn't it?

I know, I hear you... it's all easier said than done? A lot of what's going on in the world doesn't feel like a miracle at all. Sometimes it seems like suffering will choke the life right out of us.

But that's why you practice. That's why you can't tame joy, make it behave, keep it existing when and where you think it should.

Joy needs to be wild. It is wild.

In the Torah, Simcha (joy) was not an individual experience, it had a collective quality. It's not something to be achieved, but something to be shared. For the Ancient Hebrews, joy was a collective experience. Even the Psalms express joy as being an exchange between the Divine and God's beloved. For us to practice joy, we must practice it together.

The great Indian poet, Rabindranath Tagore once said: *"I slept and dreamt that life was joy. I awoke and saw that life was service. I acted and behold, service was joy."*

Mindful Prompt: If you struggle to find and feel joy, practice it. Think of something you love that makes you happy, that brings you close to your true self. Make some time today to practice that experience. And when you do, savour it. Be present in it and to it. Follow where it leads. Drink it up. Let it run wild.

ReWILD YOUR JOY. LET IT GO FREE.
LET IT RISE UP, STRONG AND MIGHTY
AND POWERFUL.

JOY IS A WILD, WILD THING - PART 6

Let It Go Free

Joy is an act of resistance.

Joy is rebellious.

Joy is a rebel gone wild.

When Jesus said:
"Love your enemy,
bless the one who curses you,
do something wonderful for the one who hates you,
and respond to the very ones who persecute you by praying
for them." (12.)
He was telling his friends to use joy as a form of

rebellion.

When terror wants to steal your peace, revel in the beauty of the life you have. When anxiety fills your mind with static noise, seek the joy of quiet and stillness. Drop into your breath; breathe joy deep into your belly. When expectation insists you earn more and buy more and be more, rest in the truth that you are enough as you are. You don't need to chase anything for fulfilment. You already have it within you. When sickness complicates and makes everything harder, stay with it. Don't hide or numb or wish yourself away; love yourself to healing. When pain demands

retribution and vengeance, pay it back with grace and forgiveness. When the frailty of life begs you to turn your head away, hold it's face in your hands and grant the dying dignity and honour with your witness. When governments and groups and committees and institutions decide who can stay and who needs to go, throw your door wide open. Set the table. Pour the wine.

"Go home and prepare a feast, holiday food and drink; and share it with those who don't have anything: This day is holy to God. Don't feel bad. The joy of God is your strength!" (13.)

Re-wild your joy. Let it go free. Let it rise up, strong and mighty and powerful.

Because in these times, finding joy could be the most rebellious, revolutionary, and holy work you can do.

Mindful Prompt: Think of something you believe about yourself and the world - something that cultivates health and wholeness and joy. Hold that feeling in your mind and body. Use this sense of power as a foundation, even when faced with things that make you angry or sad or frustrated, bring them to the joy, show them that other things are going on, too.

JOY IS A WILD, WILD THING - PART 7
Let Yourself Be

When we hear the word wild, we think of words like untamed and dangerous and out of control and unpredictable. We seem to be okay with the word being associated with things of nature, but when it comes to humanity, wild is something we think belongs out there away from here where things are tamed and controlled and domesticated and as they should be.

But are things as they should be?

Wild is the natural state of things before anyone came along and tried to make things other than what they are.

Glennon Doyle wrote:
"Every time you pretend to be less than you are, you steal permission from other women to exist fully. Don't mistake modesty for humility. Modesty is a giggly lie. An act. A mask. A fake game. We have no time for it. The word humility derives from the Latin word humilitas, which means "of the earth." To be humble is to be grounded in knowing who you are. It implies the responsibility to become what you were meant to become, to grow, to reach, to fully bloom as high and strong and grand as you were created to. It is not honorable for a tree to wilt and shrink and disappear. It's not honorable for a woman to, either." (14.)

What is your true nature? Who are you at your most wild and free?

Sometimes it takes getting out of human-made cities and towns and homes and titles and labels and identities and going back into nature, touching the earth you were made from, to discover who you are.

Wild is dangerous because wild is brave enough to be humble. To be whatever it is, is its power and strength.

"This day is holy to our Lord. Do not grieve, for the joy of the Lord is your strength."

We've been conditioned to think that joy is the reward at the end of things if you've been good enough, and worked hard enough, and have earned it. But that's not true. Joy is here for the journey, it has been all along. It is your fuel. It is your strength to continue on. Joy is what you need. Joy will heal you. Joy is wild and free and humble and brave.

Come back to joy. Come back to the natural state of who you are: graced, loved, enough. Come back to the pure and simple joy of breathing and seeing and listening and laughing. Come home to yourself.

Re-wild your joy. Set it free. Revel in it. Practice it. Let it be.

Let yourself be.

Mindful Prompt: "Like the joy of the sea coming home to shore, may the relief of laughter rinse through your soul. As the wind loves to call things to dance, may your gravity by lightened by grace. Like the dignity of moonlight restoring the earth, may your thoughts incline with reverence and respect. As water takes whatever shape it is in, so free may you be about who you become. As silence smiles on the other side of what's said, may your sense of irony bring perspective. As time remains free of all that it frames, may your mind stay clear of all it names. May your prayer of listening deepen enough to hear in the depths the laughter of God." John O'Donohue. (15.)

REFERENCES

THERE IS MORE FOR YOU

1). Luke 6:38, TPT. BroadStreet Publishing Group LLC, 2017.
2). John 10:10, TPT. BroadStreet Publishing Group LLC, 2017.
3). Alan Cohen. How Good Can it Get? What I Learned From the Richest Man in the world. Pg. 14. Hamptons Road Publishing, 2011.
4). Brené Brown. Daring Greatly: How the Courage to Be Vulnerable Transforms the Way We Live, Love, Parent, and Lead. Penguin, 2018.
5). John 10:10,TPT. BroadStreet Publishing Group LLC, 2017.
6). Mark 4:24, MSG. NavPress, 2014.
7). John 10:10, TPT. BroadStreet Publishing Group LLC, 2017.
8). Eph 3:20, TPT. BroadStreet Publishing Group LLC, 2017.
9). John 10:10, TPT. BroadStreet Publishing Group LLC, 2017.

YOU ARE THE MIRACLE

1). Ephesians 3:21, MSG. NavPress, 2014.
2). Romans 8:28, MSG. NavPress, 2014.
3). John 2, MSG. NavPress, 2014.
4). Letters to a Young Poet, Rainer Maria Rilke. Translated by M.D. Herter Nortan. Nortan Agency, 1993.
5). In The Storm, by Mary Oliver.
6). Paulo Coelho, By the River Piedra I Sat Down and Wept: A Novel of Forgiveness. HarperOne 2009.

ACCEPT AND ALLOW

1). Phil 4:11-13, MSG. NavPress, 2014.
2). Eckhart Tolle, The Power of Now. Pg 36, New World Library, 2006.
3). Phil 4:11-13, MSG. NavPress, 2014.
4).Ps 139:2-12, MSG. NavPress, 2014.
5). Elizabeth Gilbert, www.oprah.com/inspiration/elizabeth-gilbert-how-to-transform-suffering November 2020.
6). New 8:10, NIV. Hodder and Stoughton, 2011.
7). Eckhart Tolle, Stillness Speaks. Hachette Australia, 2011.
8). Phil 4:7, MSG. NavPress, 2014.
9). Paulo Coelho, Brida. Harper Collins, 2009.
10). Ps 34:18, MSG. NavPress, 2014.
11). Phil 4:11-13, MSG. NavPress, 2014.
12). Phil 4:23, MSG. NavPress, 22014.
13). Cheryl Strayed, Wild: A Journey From Lost to Found. Atlantic Books, 2012.

COME TO YOUR SENSES

1). 1 Corinthians 15:34, TPT. Broad Street Publishing, 2016.
2). 1 Corinthians 15:34, MSG. NavPress, 2014.
3). Jeremiah 17:9, NKJV. Thomas Nelson, 2005.
4). Jeremiah 17:9, MSG. NavPress, 2014.
5). Thomas Merton, Conjectures of a Guilty Bystander. Image; Revised ed. 1968.
6). Mark 8:18, TPT. Broad Street Publishing, 2016.
7). John Philip Newell, Christ of the Celts; The Healing of Creation. Wild Goose Publications, 2016.
8). Glennon Doyle, Untamed. Vermilion, 2020.
9). Galatians 2:20, NIV. Hodder & Stoughton, 2011.
10). Matthew 16:25, TPT. Broad Street Publishing, 2016.
11). Proverbs 3:5, NIV. Hodder & Stoughton, 2011.
12). Galatians 5:17, NIV. Hodder & Stoughton, 2011.
13). Galatians 2:20, TPT. Broad Street Publishing, 2016.
14). 1 Corinthians 15:34, MSG. NavPress, 2014.
15). Eckhart Tolle, The Power of Now. Hachette Australia, 2018.

YOU WILL HEAL FROM THIS

1). Romans 12:2, MSG. NavPress, 2014.
2). Revelation 21:5, MSG. NavPress, 2014.
3). Rainer Maria Rilke, Letters to a Young Poet. Translation by M. D. Herter Norton. W. W. Norton & Company New York London.
4). Mark Nepo, The Book of Awakening. Red Wheel, 2020.
5). 2 Corinthians 12:9, MSG. NavPress, 2014.
6). Matthew 9:36, MSG. NavPress, 2014..

SAFETY FIRST

1). Ecclesiastes 7:15, CJB. Hendrickson Publishers, Inc. 2016.
2). Ps 4:8, ESV. Crossway. 2011.
3). Brené Brown, The Gifts of Imperfection. Hazelden Publishing, 2010.
4). Eze 36:26, NIV. Hodder & Stoughton, 2011.
5). Mary Oliver, New and Selected Poems, Volume 2. Beacon Press, 2006.
6). Ps 34:7, NIV. Hodder & Stoughton, 2011.
7). Prov 18:10, NIV. Hodder & Stoughton, 2011.
8). Ps 121:7-8, NIV. Hodder & Stoughton, 2011.
9). Isa 43:2, MSG. NavPress, 2014.
10). Shane Koyczan, Blueprint for a Breakthrough. 2013.
11). Frederick Buechner, Beyond Words. HarperOne, 2009.
12). Ps 20:7, NIV. Hodder & Stoughton, 2011.
13). Marianne Williamson, A Return to Love. Thorsons/Element - GB, 1996.

IMAGE CREDITS

STAND IN YOUR POWER

1). Psalm 40:2, TJSB. Oxford University Press USA, 2014.
2). John Philip Newell, Christ of Celts. Wild Goose Publications, 2008.
3). Psalm 40:2, TJSB. Oxford University Press USA, 2014.
4). Anne Lamott, Bird by Bird. Anchor, 2007.
5). Richard Rohr, The Divine Dance. SPCK, 2016.
6). Rupi Kaur, Milk and Honey. Andrews McMeel Publishing, 2016.
7). Brene Brown, Daring Greatly. Penguin Life, 2016.
8). Richard Rohr, The Divine Dance. SPCK, 2016.
9). 2 Timothy 1:7, NKJV. Thomas Nelson, 2005.
10). Habakkuk 3:19, AMP. Zondervan, 2015.

JOY IS A WILD, WILD THING

1). Nehemiah 8:10, NIV. Hodder & Stoughton, 2011.
2). Khalil Gibran, The Prophet. Penguin, 2019.
3). J.D. Salinger, Nine Stories. Little, Brown and Company, 2001.
4). Nehemiah 8:10, NIV. Hodder & Stoughton, 2011.
5). Frederick Buechner, Secrets in the Dark. HarperOne, 2009.
6). Psalm 16:11, ESV. Crossway. 2011.
7). Psalm 16:11, TPT. Broad Street Publishing, 2016.
8). Frederick Buechner, The Hungering Dark. HarperOne, 1985.
9). John O'Donohue, To Bless the Space Between Us. Crown, 2014.
10). Glennon Doyle, Untamed. Vermillion, 2020.
11). Psalm 30:5, MSG. NavPress 2014.
12). Matthew 5:44-45, TPT. Broad Street Publishing, 2016.
13). Nehemiah 8:10, NIV. Hodder & Stoughton, 2011.
14). Glennon Doyle, Untamed. Vermillion, 2020.
15). John O'Donohue, To Bless the Space Between Us. Crown, 2014.

All the incredible images throughout this book come from the generous and beautiful artists of unsplash.com (unless mentioned otherwise). Your work is beautiful and kind and generative. Even though some of you may not see this, thank you for bringing such light (and capture of light!) into the world. Your images bring these little reflections to life. In order of appearance

FRONT COVER:
Lucas Silva Pinheiro Santos

INSIDE COVER:
Quentin Lagache

LIZ PORTRAIT:
David James Photography aka "Deej"
davidjamesphoto.com.au

THERE IS MORE FOR YOU:
Amy Humphries, Annie Sprat, Rushabh Nishar, Alyson McPhee, Scott Webb, Milos Vlajkovic, Thomas Verbrug, Bogomil Mihaylov, Zachary Keimig.

CAN YOU BELIEVE:
Hiva Sharifi, Hassan Weller, Chris Lawton, Steven Su, Steven Ha, 30DaysReplay, Kristina Tamasau, Tatono.

SIT WITH IT:
Content Pixie, Mariana Beltran, Derick McKinney, Klara KuliKova, Priscilla Du-Preez, Debby Hudson, Ellen Qin, Kadet, Luisa Brimble.

COME TO YOUR SENSES:
Lucas Silva Pinheiro Santos, Darrell, Chaddock, Daniele Salutari, Filipa Campos, La So, Everson De-Souza, Taylor Simpson, Larm Rmah, Cristian Castillo.

YOU WILL HEAL FROM THIS:
The Creative Exchange, Ruslan Bardash, Ezequiel Garrido, Michel Catalisano, Tim Chow, Wesley Tingey, Catherine Chu.

HOW TO KEEP YOUR HEART SAFE:
Rui Silva Sj, Kinga Cichewicz, Adrian Xft, Homero Ochoa, Marco Chilese, Krismas, Gijs Coolen, Tito Texidor III, Hennie Stander.

BACK ON YOUR FEET:
Wesley Tingey, Gemma Evans, Eberhard Grossgasteiger, Khara Woods, Annie Spratt, Evie S, Pelayo Arbues, Pawel Czerwinski, Gaelle Marcel, Pawel Czerwinski.

RE-WILD YOUR JOY:
Chandra Oh, Annie Spratt, Daniel Squibb, Klara Kulikova, Peter Aschoff, Olga Serjantu, Kirsten Drew, Annie Spratt, Wellington Ferreira, Kyle Head.

THANK YOU PAGE:
Max Fuchs

NOTES:

THANKYOU

The best thing about The Practice Co and the journey it's been on these last eight years, is that it has led me to you. So many of you email and DM and comment with your questions and your stories and your thanks and even your push back on things you don't agree with, and I can't tell you how much it lights me up and makes me feel like I'm alive. I couldn't do this without all of you who support our work via the App. I don't have words except to say thank you all the thank you's. Because of you, and the stories that we share together, I am committed now more than ever to create a space of spiritual practice that is healthy and organic and life-giving, free of platitudes and manipulation and ridiculous standards of purity and success and image. You have received me so generously into your heart and life, and I will live out my days so grateful for it.

So much thanks to my family and friends who are constantly challenging me to be bigger and braver while at the same time helping me love myself and embrace this journey. Friendship has saved my life, and I'm grateful for you all. Gratitude, as always, to my partner and love, Jesse Milani. What a ride. And there's so much more we are yet to experience. I'm so glad I get to experience it with you. Sam and Bree and Oli, you make me better. I love you. Go to bed. Huge thanks to my girl Jessamy, who answered a desperate call and designed this beautiful book you hold in your hands. Babe. Honestly. You are too much, and I'm so grateful. Thanks to my many mentors from afar, you don't know how much you have shaped and changed my life - Jen Hatmaker, Rob Bell, Liz Gilbert, Nicole Sachs, Sarah Bessey, Richard Rohr, Mary Oliver, Rilke, Rumi, Ram Dass, Glennon Doyle. I know you know your work matters, but your work matters, and it helps people beyond what you know and can imagine, and it's beautiful and powerful, and I'm so grateful.

And finally, gratitude to the ever-loving, creative energy, Divine, God, the source of all things, the ground of being, the endlessly knowable one... I feel like I know less and less about you, but this makes me know you and who and what and why you are, all the more, and all the more graciously and lovingly, too. Let's play. I'm ready.

Liz
xy

CPSIA information can be obtained
at www.ICGtesting.com
Printed in the USA
BVHW021013120122
626005BV00009B/127